Barbecue

200 recipes for outdoor eating

Barbecue

Consultant editor: Christine France

southwater

This edition is published by Southwater

Distributed in the UK by
The Manning Partnership
251–253 London Road East
Batheaston
Bath BA1 7RL
UK
tel. (0044) 01225 852 727
fax (0044) 01225 852 852

Distributed in Australia by
Sandstone Publishing
Unit 1, 360 Norton Street
Leichhardt
New South Wales 2040
Australia
tel. (0061) 2 9560 7888
fax (0061) 2 9560 7488

Distributed in New Zealand by
Five Mile Press NZ
PO Box 33-1071
Takapuna
Auckland 9
New Zealand
tel. (0064) 9 4444 144
fax (0064) 9 4444 518

Southwater is an imprint of Anness Publishing Limited
© 1998, 2000 Anness Publishing Limited

1 3 5 7 9 10 8 6 4 2

Publisher: Joanna Lorenz
Project Editor: Sarah Ainley
Copy Editor: Beverley Jollands
Designer: Nigel Partridge
Jacket Illustration and Design: Clare Baggaley
Illustrations: Madeleine David and Lucinda Ganderton
Photographers: Karl Adamson, William Adams-Lingwood, Edward Allwright,
Steve Baxter, James Duncan, John Freeman, Michelle Garrett, Amanda Heywood,
Don Last, Michael Michaels, Patrick McLeavey, Debbie Patterson and Juliet Piddington
Recipes: Carla Capalbo, Jacqueline Clark, Carole Clements, Roz Denny, Nicola Diggins,
Tessa Evelegh, Joanna Farrow, Christine France, Silvana Franco, Soheila Kimberley,
Ruby Le Bois, Sue Maggs, Katherine Richmond, Steven Wheeler and Elizabeth Wolf-Cohen

For all recipes, quantities are given in both metric and imperial measures,
and, where appropriate, measures are also given in standard cups and spoons.
Follow one set, but not a mixture, because they are not interchangeable.

Previously published as *The Ultimate Barbecue Cookbook*

CONTENTS

· · ·

INTRODUCTION

However simple, there's something about the char-grilled flavour of barbecued food that makes it taste extra special. Maybe it owes part of its appeal to the fresh air that sharpens the appetite and makes that tantalizing aroma so totally irresistible.

There's nothing new about cooking over charcoal; in fact, it's a method of cooking that has been used in most civilizations throughout history. The basic method has changed little over the centuries, but many modern barbecues are very sophisticated, making the job easier, cleaner and more controllable. Whether you're cooking over a simple pile of sticks or on a top-of-the-range barbecue, outdoor cooking is fun, easy and inexpensive.

There are disputes over the origin of the word barbecue, but one explanation is that it comes from *barbacoa*, an American-Spanish word used by the Arawak tribe of the Caribbean, as the name for the wooden frame that held their food over an open fire as it cooked. The Arawaks were cannibals, so the food we cook today is rather different from their offerings!

Whatever your tastes, this collection of recipes offers new, unusual ideas for your barbecue as well as some traditional favourites. There's something for every occasion, from family meals to entertaining: spicy, fruity and exotic grills using fish, meat and poultry; easy sauces and marinades to turn basic ingredients into something new and special; and luscious, indulgent desserts. For vegetarians, there's a whole chapter of innovative ideas that everyone will enjoy.

Best of all, not only does a barbecue set the cook free from the kitchen but, for once, everyone else will actually want to help with the cooking.

CHOOSING A BARBECUE
. . .

There is a huge choice of ready-made barbecues on the market, and it's important to choose one that suits your needs. First decide how many people you want to cook for and where you are likely to use the barbecue. For instance, do you usually have barbecues just for the family, or are you likely to have barbecue parties for lots of friends? Once you've decided on your basic requirements, you will be able to choose between the different types more easily.

Hibachi Barbecues
These small cast-iron barbecues originated in Japan – the word *hibachi* translates literally as 'firebox'. They are inexpensive, easy to use and easily transportable. Lightweight versions are now made in steel or aluminium.

ABOVE: *Hibachi barbecue*

Disposable Barbecues
These will last for about an hour and are a convenient idea for picnic-style barbecues or for cooking just a few small pieces of food.

Portable Barbecues
These are usually quite light and fold away to fit into a car boot so you can take them on picnics. Some are even small enough to fit into a rucksack.

Brazier Barbecues
These open barbecues are suitable for use on a patio or in the garden. Most have legs or wheels and it's a good idea to check that the height suits you. The grill

area of a brazier barbecue varies in size and the barbecue may be round or rectangular. It's useful to choose one that has a shelf attached to the side. Other extras may include an electric, battery-powered or clockwork spit: choose one on which you can adjust the height of the spit. Many brazier barbecues have a hood, which is useful as a windbreak and gives a place to mount the spit.

LEFT: *Brazier barbecue*
BELOW: *Disposable barbecue*
RIGHT: *Portable barbecue*

ABOVE: Gas barbecue

Kettle-grill Barbecues

These have a large, hinged lid which can be used as a windbreak; when closed, the lid allows you to use the barbecue rather like an oven. Even large joints of meat or whole turkeys cook successfully, as the heat reflected within the dome helps to brown the meat evenly. The heat is easily controlled by the use of efficient air vents. This type of barbecue can also be used for home-smoking foods.

Gas Barbecues

The main advantage of these is their convenience – the heat is instant and easily controllable. The disadvantage is that they tend to be quite expensive.

Permanent Barbecues

These are a good idea if you often have barbecues at home. They can be built simply and cheaply. Choose a sheltered site that is a little way from the house, but with easy access to the kitchen. Permanent barbecues can be built with

ordinary house bricks, but it's best to line the inside with firebricks, which will withstand the heat better. Use a metal shelf for the fuel and a grid at whatever height you choose. Packs are available containing all you need to build a barbecue.

Improvised Barbecues

Barbecue cooking adds to the fun of eating outdoors on picnics and camping trips but transporting the barbecue for the rest of the day can make the idea more of a chore than a treat. Basic barbecues can be built at almost no cost and can be dismantled after use as quickly as they were put together. A pile of stones topped with chicken wire and fuelled with driftwood or kindling makes a very efficient barbecue. Or take a large biscuit tin with you and punch a few holes in it; fill it with charcoal and place a grid on top. With just a little planning, you can turn your trip into a truly memorable event.

ABOVE: Improvised barbecue

ABOVE: Permanent barbecue

TYPES OF FUEL

· · ·

If you have a gas or electric barbecue, you will not need to buy extra fuel, but other barbecues require either charcoal or wood. Choose good-quality fuel from sustainable sources, and always store it in a dry place.

Lumpwood Charcoal
Lumpwood charcoal is usually made from softwood, and comes in lumps of varying size. It is easier to ignite than briquettes, but tends to burn up faster.

Charcoal Briquettes
Briquettes are a cost-effective choice of fuel as they burn for a long time with the minimum of smell and smoke. They can take a long time to ignite, however.

ABOVE: *Charcoal briquettes*

Self-igniting Charcoal
This is simply lumpwood charcoal or briquettes, treated with a flammable substance that catches light very easily. It's important to wait until the ignition agent has burnt off before cooking food, or the smell may taint the food.

Coconut-shell Charcoal
This makes a good fuel for small barbecues. It's best used on a fire grate with small holes, as the small pieces tend to fall through the gaps.

Wood
Hardwoods such as oak and olive are best for barbecues, as they burn slowly with a pleasant aroma. Softwoods tend to burn too fast and give off sparks and smoke, making them unsuitable for most barbecues. Wood fires need constant attention to achieve an even, steady heat.

BELOW: *Lumpwood*

CONTROLLING THE HEAT
There are three basic ways to control the heat of the barbecue during cooking.

1 Adjust the height of the grill rack. Raise it for slow cooking, or use the bottom level for searing foods. For a medium heat, the rack should be about 10cm/4in from the fire.

2 Push the burning coals apart for a lower heat; pile them closer together to increase the heat of the fire.

3 Most barbecues have air vents to allow air into the fire. Open them to make the fire hotter, or close them to lower the temperature.

Woodchips and Herbs
These are designed to be added to the fire to impart a pleasant aroma to the food. They can be soaked to make them last longer. Scatter woodchips and herbs straight on to the coals during cooking, or place them on a metal tray under the grill rack. Packs of hickory or oak chips are easily available, or you can simply scatter twigs of juniper, rosemary, thyme, sage or fennel over the fire.

BELOW: *Coconut shell*

LIGHTING THE FIRE
Follow these basic instructions for lighting the fire unless you are using self-igniting charcoal, in which case you should follow the manu-facturer's instructions.

1 Spread a layer of foil over the base of the barbecue, to reflect the heat and make cleaning easier.

2 Spread a layer of wood, charcoal or briquettes on the fire grate about 5cm/2in deep. Pile the fuel in a small pyramid in the centre.

3 Push one or two firelighters into the pyramid or pour over about 45ml/3 tbsp liquid firelighter and leave for 1 minute. Light with a long match or taper and leave to burn for 15 minutes. Spread the coals evenly and leave for 30–45 minutes, until they are covered with a film of grey ash, before cooking.

SAFETY TIPS

∘ ∘ ∘

Barbecuing is a perfectly safe method of cooking if it's done sensibly – use these simple guidelines as a basic checklist to safeguard against accidents. If you have never organized a barbecue before, keep your first few attempts as simple as possible, with just one or two types of food. When you have mastered the technique of cooking on a barbecue you can start to become more ambitious. Soon you will progress from burgers for two to meals for large parties of family and friends.

☆ Make sure the barbecue is sited on a firm surface and is stable and level before lighting the fire. Once the barbecue is lit, do not move it.

☆ Keep the barbecue sheltered from the wind, and keep it well away from trees and shrubs.

☆ Always follow the manufacturer's instructions for your barbecue, as there are some barbecues that can use only one type of fuel.

☆ Don't try to hasten the fire – some fuels may take quite a time to build up heat. Never pour flammable liquid on to the barbecue.

☆ Keep children and pets away from the fire and make sure the cooking is always supervised by adults.

☆ Keep perishable foods cold until you're ready to cook – especially in hot weather. If you take them outdoors, place them in a cool bag until needed.

☆ Make sure meats such as burgers, sausages and poultry are thoroughly cooked – there should be no trace of pink in the juices. Pierce a thick part of flesh as a test: the juices should run clear.

RIGHT: Poultry can be pre-cooked in the oven or microwave, before being finished off on the barbecue.

ABOVE: Light the fire with a long match or taper, and leave it to burn for about 15 minutes.

☆ Wash your hands after handling raw meat and before touching other foods. Don't use the same utensils for raw ingredients and cooked food.

☆ You may prefer to pre-cook poultry in the microwave or oven and then transfer it to the barbecue to finish off cooking and to attain the flavour of barbecued food. Don't allow meat to cool down before transferring it to the barbecue; poultry should never be reheated once it has cooled.

☆ In case the fire should get out of control, have a bucket of sand and a water spray on hand to douse the flames.

☆ Keep a first-aid kit handy. If someone burns themselves, hold the burn under cold running water.

☆ Trim excess fat from meat and don't use too much oil in marinades. Fat can cause dangerous flare-ups if too much is allowed to drip on to the fuel.

☆ Use long-handled barbecue tools, such as forks, tongs and brushes, for turning and basting food; keep some oven gloves to hand, preferably the extra-long type, to protect your hands.

☆ Always keep the raw foods to be cooked away from foods that are ready to eat, to prevent cross-contamination.

BASIC TIMING GUIDE

· · ·

It is almost impossible to give precise timing guides for barbecue cooking as there are so many factors to consider. The heat will depend on the type and size of barbecue, the type of fuel used, the height of the grill above the fire and, of course, the weather. Cooking times will also be affected by the thickness and type of food, the quality of the meat, and whereabouts on the grill it is placed.

Bearing this in mind, the chart below provides only a rough guide to timing. Food should always be tested to make sure it is thoroughly cooked. The times given here are total cooking times, allowing for the food to be turned. Most foods need turning only once but smaller items, such as kebabs and sausages, need to be turned more frequently to ensure even cooking. Foods wrapped in foil cook more slowly and will need longer on the barbecue.

TYPE OF FOOD	WEIGHT/ THICKNESS	HEAT	TOTAL COOKING TIME
BEEF			
steaks	2.5cm/1in	hot	rare: 5 minutes
			medium: 8 minutes
			well done: 12 minutes
burgers	2cm/¾ in	hot	6–8 minutes
kebabs	2.5cm/1in	hot	5–8 minutes
joints	1.5kg/3½ lb	spit	2–3 hours
LAMB			
leg steaks	2cm/¾ in	medium	10–15 minutes
chops	2.5cm/1in	medium	10–15 minutes
kebabs	2.5cm/1in	medium	6–15 minutes
butterfly leg	7.5cm/3in	low	rare: 40–45 minutes
			well done: 1 hour
rolled shoulder	1.5kg/3½ lb	spit	1¼–1½ hours
PORK			
chops	2.5cm/1in	medium	15–18 minutes
kebabs	2.5cm/1in	medium	12–15 minutes
spare ribs		medium	30–40 minutes
sausages	thick	medium	8–10 minutes
joints	1.5kg/3½ lb	spit	2–3 hours

TYPE OF FOOD	WEIGHT/ THICKNESS	HEAT	TOTAL COOKING TIME
CHICKEN			
whole	1.5kg/3½ lb	spit	1–1¼ hours
quarters		medium	30–35 minutes
boneless breasts		medium	10–15 minutes
drumsticks		medium	25–30 minutes
kebabs		medium	6–10 minutes
poussin, whole	450g/1lb	spit	25–30 minutes
poussin, spatchcocked	450g/1lb	medium	25–30 minutes
DUCKLING			
whole	2.25kg/5lb	spit	1–1½ hours
half		medium	35–45 minutes
breasts, boneless		medium	15–20 minutes
FISH			
large, whole	2.25–4.5kg/ 5–10lb	low/ medium	allow 10 minutes per 2.5cm/1in thickness
small, whole	500–900g/ 1¼–2lb	hot/ medium	12–20 minutes
sardines		hot/ medium	4–6 minutes
steaks or fillets	2.5cm/1in	medium	6–10 minutes
kebabs	2.5cm/1in	medium	5–8 minutes
large prawns in shell		medium	6–8 minutes
large prawns, shelled		medium	4–6 minutes
scallops/mussels in shell		medium	until open
scallops/mussels, shelled, skewered		medium	5–8 minutes
half lobster		low/ medium	15–20 minutes

MARINATING

· ○ ○

Marinades are used to add flavour and to moisten or tenderize foods, particularly meat. Marinades can be either savoury or sweet and are as varied as you want to make them: spicy, fruity, fragrant or exotic. Certain classic combinations always work well with certain foods. Usually, it is best to choose oily marinades for dry foods, such as lean meat or white fish, and wine- or vinegar-based marinades for rich foods with a higher fat content. Most marinades don't contain salt, which can draw out the juices from meat. It's better to add salt just before, or after, cooking.

1 Place the food for marinating in a wide, non-metallic dish or bowl, preferably a dish that is large enough to allow the food to lie in a single layer.

2 Mix together the ingredients for the marinade according to the recipe. The marinade can usually be prepared in advance and stored in a jar with a screw-top lid until needed.

3 Pour the marinade over the food and turn the food to coat it evenly.

4 Cover the dish or bowl with clear film and chill in the fridge for anything from 30 minutes up to several hours or overnight, depending on the recipe. Turn the food over occasionally and spoon the marinade over it to ensure it is well coated.

5 Remove the food with a slotted spoon, or lift it out with tongs, and drain off and reserve the marinade. If necessary, allow the food to come to room temperature before cooking.

6 Use the marinade for basting or brushing the food during cooking.

Cook's Tip

The amount of marinade you will need depends on the amount of food. As a rough guide, about 150ml/¼ pint/⅔ cup is enough for about 500g/1¼ lb of food.

BASIC BARBECUE MARINADE

This can be used for meat or fish.

1 garlic clove, crushed
45ml/3 tbsp sunflower or olive oil
45ml/3 tbsp dry sherry
15ml/1 tbsp Worcestershire sauce
15ml/1 tbsp dark soy sauce
freshly ground black pepper

RED WINE MARINADE

This is good with red meats and game.

150ml/¼ pint/⅔ cup dry red wine
15ml/1 tbsp olive oil
15ml/1 tbsp red wine vinegar
2 garlic cloves, crushed
2 dried bay leaves, crumbled
freshly ground black pepper

BELOW: *Marinating foods before cooking adds to the flavour and ensures the food is kept tender and moist.*

STARTERS AND SNACKS

As everyone knows, there is nothing like the aroma of char-grilling food

to whet the appetite. To keep your guests happy while they are waiting

for the main event, begin your barbecue feast with exciting appetizers

that are quick to cook and fun to eat. Here is a collection of

flavoursome and colourful dishes that are guaranteed to disappear

from the grill rack as soon as they're cool enough to snatch away.

There are lots of creative recipes for finger foods to be nibbled with

drinks – from crisp potato skins to spicy spare ribs – with plenty of

interesting dips and sauces to dunk them in, as well as delicious

suggestions for elegant starters for more formal meals.

ROASTED GARLIC TOASTS

*Barbecuing garlic in its skin produces a soft, aromatic purée with a sweet, nutty flavour.
Spread on crisp toast to make a delicious starter or accompaniment to meat or vegetable dishes.*

INGREDIENTS

*2 whole garlic heads
extra virgin olive oil
fresh rosemary sprigs
ciabatta loaf or thick baguette
chopped fresh rosemary
salt and freshly ground black
pepper*

SERVES 4

1 Slice the tops from the heads of garlic, using a sharp kitchen knife.

2 Brush the garlic heads with extra virgin olive oil and add a few sprigs of fresh rosemary, before wrapping in kitchen foil. Cook the foil parcels on a medium-hot barbecue for about 25–30 minutes, turning occasionally, until the garlic is soft.

3 Slice the bread and brush each slice generously with olive oil. Toast the slices on the barbecue until crisp and golden, turning once.

4 Squeeze the garlic cloves from their skins on to the toasts. Sprinkle with the chopped fresh rosemary and olive oil, and add salt and black pepper to taste.

ROASTED PEPPER ANTIPASTO

. . .

Jars of Italian mixed peppers in olive oil are a common sight in supermarkets, yet none can compete with this freshly made version, perfect as a starter or served with salami and cold meats.

INGREDIENTS
3 red peppers
2 yellow or orange peppers
2 green peppers
50g/2oz/½ cup sun-dried tomatoes
in oil, drained
1 garlic clove
30ml/2 tbsp balsamic vinegar
75ml/5 tbsp olive oil
few drops of chilli sauce
4 canned artichoke hearts, drained
and sliced
salt and freshly ground black
pepper
fresh basil leaves, to garnish

SERVES 6

1 Cook the whole peppers on a medium-hot barbecue, turning frequently, for about 10–15 minutes until they begin to char. Cover the peppers with a clean dish towel and leave to cool for 5 minutes.

2 Use a sharp kitchen knife to slice the sun-dried tomatoes into thin strips. Thinly slice the garlic clove.

3 Beat together the balsamic vinegar, olive oil and chilli sauce in a small bowl, then season with a little salt and freshly ground black pepper.

4 Stalk and slice the peppers. Mix with the sliced artichokes, sun-dried tomatoes and garlic. Pour over the dressing and scatter with basil leaves.

17

HERB-STUFFED MINI VEGETABLES

These little hors d'oeuvres are ideal for parties as they can be prepared in advance, and simply assembled and cooked at the last minute.

INGREDIENTS

30 mini vegetables: courgettes, patty pan squashes and large button mushrooms
30ml/2 tbsp olive oil
fresh basil or parsley, to garnish

FOR THE STUFFING

30ml/2 tbsp olive oil
1 onion, finely chopped
1 garlic clove, finely chopped
115g/4oz button mushrooms, finely chopped
1 courgette, finely chopped
1 red pepper, finely chopped
65g/2¹/₂ oz/¹/₃ cup orzo pasta or long grain rice
90ml/6 tbsp/¹/₃ cup passata
2.5ml/¹/₂ tsp dried thyme
120ml/4fl oz/¹/₂ cup chicken stock
5–10ml/1–2 tsp chopped fresh basil or parsley
50g/2oz mozzarella or fontina cheese, coarsely grated
salt and freshly ground black pepper

MAKES 30

1 For the stuffing, heat the oil over a medium heat in a pan. Add the onion and cook for 2 minutes until tender. Stir in the garlic, mushrooms, courgette and red pepper. Season and cook for 2 minutes until the vegetables soften.

2 Stir in the pasta or rice, the passata, thyme and stock and bring to the boil, stirring. Reduce the heat and simmer for 10–12 minutes until reduced and thickened. Remove from the heat and cool slightly. Stir in the basil or parsley and the cheese.

3 Drop the courgettes and squashes into boiling water and cook for 3 minutes. Drain and refresh under cold running water. Trim the bottoms so they are flat, trim a small slice off the tops and scoop out the centres with a spoon or melon baller. Remove the stems from the mushrooms. Brush all the vegetables with olive oil.

4 Using a teaspoon, fill the vegetables with the stuffing and arrange on a rack. Grill over a medium-hot barbecue or grill for 10–15 minutes until the filling is hot and bubbling. Garnish with the fresh basil or parsley. The vegetables can be served either warm or cool.

POLPETTES WITH MOZZARELLA AND TOMATO

° ° °

These Italian-style meatballs are made with beef and topped with creamy melted mozzarella and savoury anchovies.

INGREDIENTS

½ slice white bread, crusts removed
45ml/3 tbsp milk
675g/1½ lb minced beef
1 egg, beaten
50g/2oz/⅔ cup dry breadcrumbs
olive oil for brushing
2 beefsteak or other large tomatoes, sliced
15ml/1 tbsp chopped fresh oregano
1 mozzarella cheese, cut into 6 slices
6 drained, canned anchovy fillets, cut in half lengthways
salt and freshly ground black pepper

SERVES 6

1 Put the bread and milk into a small saucepan and heat very gently, until the bread absorbs all the milk. Mash it to a pulp and set aside to cool.

2 Put the minced beef into a bowl with the bread mixture and the egg and season with plenty of salt and freshly ground black pepper. Mix well, then shape the mixture into six patties, using your hands. Sprinkle the breadcrumbs on to a plate and dredge the patties, coating them thoroughly.

3 Brush the polpettes with olive oil and cook them on a hot barbecue for 2–3 minutes on one side, until brown. Turn them over.

4 Without removing the polpettes from the barbecue, lay a slice of tomato on top of each polpette, sprinkle with chopped oregano and season with salt and pepper. Place a mozzarella slice on top and arrange two strips of anchovy in a cross over the cheese.

5 Cook for a further 4–5 minutes until the polpettes are cooked through and the mozzarella has melted.

STUFFED KIBBEH

. . .

Kibbeh is a tasty Middle Eastern speciality of minced lamb and bulgar wheat, which can be eaten raw or shaped into patties and cooked on the barbecue.

INGREDIENTS
450g/1lb lean lamb
45ml/3 tbsp olive oil
avocado slices and fresh coriander sprigs, to serve

FOR THE KIBBEH
225g/8oz/1⅓ cups bulgur wheat
1 red chilli, seeded and roughly chopped
1 onion, roughly chopped
salt and freshly ground black pepper

FOR THE STUFFING
1 onion, finely chopped
50g/2oz/⅔ cup pine nuts
30ml/2 tbsp olive oil
7.5ml/1½ tsp ground allspice
60ml/4 tbsp chopped fresh coriander

SERVES 4–6

1 Roughly cut the lamb into chunks, using a heavy kitchen knife. Process the chunks in a blender or food processor until finely minced. Divide the minced meat into two equal portions and set aside until needed.

2 To make the kibbeh, soak the bulgur wheat for 15 minutes in cold water. Drain well, then process in the blender or food processor with the chopped chilli and onion, half the meat and plenty of salt and pepper.

3 To make the stuffing, fry the onion and pine nuts in the olive oil for 5 minutes. Add the allspice and remaining minced meat and fry gently, breaking up the meat with a wooden spoon, until browned. Stir in the coriander and a little seasoning.

4 Turn the kibbeh mixture out on to a clean work surface and use your hands to shape the mixture into a cake. Divide the cake into 12 wedges.

5 Flatten one wedge in the palm of your hand and spoon a little stuffing into the centre. Bring the edges of the kibbeh over the stuffing to enclose it. Make into a firm egg-shaped mould between the palms of your hands, ensuring that the filling is completely encased. Repeat with the other kibbeh.

6 To barbecue the kibbeh, lightly brush with olive oil and cook on a medium barbecue for 10–15 minutes, turning carefully, until evenly browned and cooked through. To fry the kibbeh, heat oil to a depth of 5cm/2in in a large pan until a few kibbeh crumbs sizzle on the surface. Lower half the kibbeh into the oil and fry for about 5 minutes until golden. Drain on kitchen paper and keep hot while frying the remainder. Serve hot with avocado slices and fresh coriander sprigs.

HERB POLENTA

○ ○ ○

Golden polenta with fresh summer herbs makes an appetizing starter or light snack, served with barbecued tomatoes.

INGREDIENTS

750ml/1¼ pints/3 cups stock or water
5ml/1 tsp salt
175g/6oz/1 cup polenta
25g/1oz/2 tbsp butter
75ml/5 tbsp mixed chopped fresh parsley, chives and basil, plus extra to garnish
olive oil for brushing
4 large plum or beef tomatoes, halved
salt and freshly ground black pepper

SERVES 4

3 Remove from the heat and stir in the butter, chopped herbs and pepper.

4 Lightly grease a wide tin or dish and tip the polenta into it, spreading it evenly. Leave until cool and set.

1 Prepare the polenta in advance: place the stock or water in a saucepan, with the salt, and bring to the boil. Reduce the heat and stir in the polenta.

2 Stir constantly over a moderate heat for 5 minutes, until the polenta begins to thicken and come away from the sides of the saucepan.

5 Turn out the polenta and cut into squares or stamp out rounds with a large biscuit cutter. Brush with olive oil. Lightly brush the tomatoes with oil and sprinkle with salt and pepper. Cook the tomatoes and polenta on a medium-hot barbecue for about 5 minutes, turning once. Serve garnished with fresh herbs.

Cook's Tip

Try using fresh basil or fresh chives alone, for a distinctive flavour.

BRIE PARCELS WITH ALMONDS

∘ ∘ ∘

Creamy French Brie makes a sophisticated starter or light meal, wrapped in vine leaves and served hot with chunks of crusty bread.

2 Cut the Brie into four chunks and place each chunk on a vine leaf.

3 Mix together the chives, ground almonds, peppercorns and olive oil, and place a spoonful on top of each piece of cheese. Sprinkle with flaked almonds.

4 Fold the vine leaves over tightly to enclose the cheese completely. Brush the parcels with olive oil and cook on a hot barbecue for about 3–4 minutes, until the cheese is hot and melting. Serve immediately.

INGREDIENTS

4 large vine leaves, preserved in brine
200g/7oz piece Brie cheese
30ml/2 tbsp chopped fresh chives
30ml/2 tbsp ground almonds
5ml/1 tsp crushed black peppercorns
15ml/1 tbsp olive oil
flaked almonds

SERVES 4

1 Rinse the vine leaves thoroughly under cold running water and dry them well. Spread the leaves out on a clean work surface or chopping board.

TOFU STEAKS

∘ ∘ ∘

Vegetarians and meat-eaters alike will enjoy these barbecued tofu steaks. The combination of ingredients in the marinade gives the steaks a distinctly Japanese flavour.

INGREDIENTS

1 packet fresh tofu (10 × 8 × 3cm/ 4 × 3¼ × 1¼ in), 300g/11oz drained weight
2 spring onions, thinly sliced, to garnish
mixed salad leaves, to garnish

FOR THE MARINADE
45ml/3 tbsp sake
30ml/2 tbsp soy sauce
5ml/1 tsp sesame oil
1 garlic clove, crushed
15ml/1 tbsp grated fresh root ginger
1 spring onion, finely chopped

SERVES 4

1 Wrap the tofu in a clean dish towel and place it on a chopping board. Put a large plate on top and leave the tofu for 30 minutes to remove any excess water.

2 Slice the tofu horizontally into three pieces, then cut the slices into quarters. Set aside. Mix the ingredients for the marinade in a large bowl. Add the tofu to the bowl in a single layer and allow to marinate for 30 minutes. Drain the tofu steaks and reserve the marinade to use for basting.

3 Cook the steaks on the barbecue for 3 minutes on each side, basting regularly with the marinade, or fry them for 3 minutes in a large pan.

4 Arrange three tofu steaks on each plate. Any remaining marinade can be heated in a pan and then poured over the steaks. Sprinkle with the spring onions and garnish with mixed salad leaves. Serve immediately.

Cook's Tip
Tofu is easily obtainable from supermarkets and health food stores, and is an ideal alternative to meat.

GRILLED ASPARAGUS WITH SALT-CURED HAM

· · ·

Barbecued asparagus has a wonderfully intense flavour that stands up well to the wrapping of crisp, salty ham. Serve this traditional tapas dish with drinks before a meal.

INGREDIENTS

6 slices of serrano ham
12 asparagus spears
15ml/1 tbsp olive oil
sea salt and coarsely ground black pepper

SERVES 4

1 Halve each slice of ham lengthways and wrap one half around each of the asparagus spears.

2 Brush the ham and asparagus lightly with olive oil and sprinkle with salt and pepper. Cook on a medium barbecue for about 4 minutes, turning frequently, until the asparagus is tender but still firm. Serve at once.

Cook's Tip

If you can't find serrano ham, try using Italian prosciutto or Portuguese presunto.

POTATO SKINS WITH CAJUN DIP

· · ·

As an alternative to deep-frying, barbecuing potato skins crisps them up in no time and gives them a wonderful char-grilled flavour. This spicy dip makes the perfect partner.

INGREDIENTS

*4 large baking potatoes
olive oil for brushing
250ml/8fl oz/1 cup natural yogurt
2 garlic cloves, crushed
10ml/2 tsp tomato paste
5ml/1 tsp green chilli paste or
1 small green chilli, chopped
2.5ml/¹/2 tsp celery salt
salt and freshly ground black
pepper*

SERVES 4

1 Bake or microwave the potatoes until tender. Cut them in half and scoop out the flesh, leaving a thin layer of potato on the skins. The scooped out potato can be reserved in the fridge or freezer for another meal.

2 Cut each potato shell in half again and lightly brush the skins with olive oil. Cook on a medium-hot barbecue for 4–5 minutes, or until crisp.

3 Mix together the remaining ingredients in a bowl to make the dip. Serve the potato skins with the Cajun dip on the side.

Cook's Tip
If you don't have any chilli paste or fresh chillies, add one or two drops of hot pepper sauce to the dip instead.

SPICY CHICKEN WINGS

· · ·

These deliciously sticky bites will appeal to adults and children alike, although younger eaters might prefer a little less chilli.

INGREDIENTS

8 plump chicken wings
2 large garlic cloves, cut into slivers
15ml/1 tbsp olive oil
15ml/1 tbsp paprika
5ml/1 tsp chilli powder
5ml/1 tsp dried oregano
salt and freshly ground black pepper
lime wedges, to serve

SERVES 4

1 Using a small sharp kitchen knife, make one or two cuts in the skin of each chicken wing and slide a sliver of garlic under the skin. Brush the wings generously with the olive oil.

2 In a large bowl, stir together the paprika, chilli powder and oregano and season with plenty of salt and pepper. Add the chicken wings and toss together until very lightly coated in the mixture.

3 Cook the chicken wings on a medium barbecue for 15 minutes until they are cooked through, with a blackened, crispy skin. Serve with fresh lime wedges to squeeze over.

CHICKEN WINGS TERIYAKI STYLE

○ ○ ○

This oriental glaze is very simple to prepare and adds a unique flavour to the meat. The glaze can be used with any cut of chicken or with fish.

INGREDIENTS

1 garlic clove, crushed
45ml/3 tbsp soy sauce
30ml/2 tbsp dry sherry
10ml/2 tsp clear honey
10ml/2 tsp grated fresh root ginger
5ml/1 tsp sesame oil
12 chicken wings
15ml/1 tbsp sesame seeds, toasted

SERVES 4

1 Place the garlic, soy sauce, sherry, honey, grated ginger and sesame oil in a large bowl and beat with a fork, to mix the ingredients together evenly.

2 Add the chicken wings and toss thoroughly, to coat in the marinade. Cover the bowl with clear film and chill for about 30 minutes, or longer.

3 Cook the chicken wings on a fairly hot barbecue for about 20–25 minutes, turning occasionally and basting with the remaining marinade.

4 Sprinkle the chicken wings with sesame seeds. Serve the wings on their own as a starter or side dish, or with a crisp green salad.

SKEWERED LAMB WITH RED ONION SALSA

° · °

*A simple salsa makes a refreshing accompaniment to this summery dish – make sure you use a
mild-flavoured red onion that is fresh and crisp, and a tomato that is ripe and full of flavour.*

INGREDIENTS
*225g/8oz lean lamb, cubed
2.5ml/½ tsp ground cumin
5ml/1 tsp ground paprika
15ml/1 tbsp olive oil
salt and freshly ground black
pepper*

FOR THE SALSA
*1 red onion, very thinly sliced
1 large tomato, seeded and
chopped
15ml/1 tbsp red wine vinegar
3–4 fresh basil or mint leaves,
roughly torn
small mint leaves, to garnish*

SERVES 4

1 Place the lamb in a large bowl with
the cumin, paprika and olive oil and
season with plenty of salt and freshly
ground black pepper. Toss well. Cover
the bowl with clear film and leave in
a cool place for several hours, or in the
fridge overnight, so that the lamb fully
absorbs the spicy flavours.

2 Spear the lamb cubes on four small
skewers. If using wooden skewers, soak
them first in cold water for at least 30
minutes to prevent them burning when
placed on the barbecue.

3 To make the salsa, put the sliced
onion, tomato, red wine vinegar and
torn fresh basil or mint leaves in a
small bowl and stir together until
thoroughly blended. Season to taste
with salt and garnish with mint.

4 Cook the skewered lamb on a
hot barbecue, or under a hot grill,
for about 5–10 minutes, turning the
skewers frequently, until the lamb is
well browned but still slightly pink in
the centre. Serve hot, with the salsa.

SPICY MEATBALLS
· · ·

These meatballs are delicious served piping hot with chilli sauce. Keep the sauce on the side so that everyone can add as much heat as they like.

2 Add the minced beef, shallots, garlic, breadcrumbs, beaten egg and parsley, with plenty of salt and pepper. Mix well, then use your hands to shape the mixture into 18 small balls.

3 Brush the meatballs with olive oil and cook on a medium barbecue, or fry them in a large pan, for about 10–15 minutes, turning regularly until evenly browned and cooked through.

INGREDIENTS

115g/4oz fresh spicy sausages
115g/4oz minced beef
2 shallots, finely chopped
2 garlic cloves, finely chopped
75g/3oz/1½ cups fresh white breadcrumbs
1 egg, beaten
30ml/2 tbsp chopped fresh parsley, plus extra to garnish
15ml/1 tbsp olive oil
salt and freshly ground black pepper
Tabasco or other hot chilli sauce, to serve

SERVES 6

1 Use your hands to remove the skins from the spicy sausages, placing the sausagemeat in a mixing bowl and breaking it up with a fork.

4 Transfer the meatballs to a warm dish and sprinkle with chopped fresh parsley. Serve with chilli sauce.

FIVE-SPICE RIB-STICKERS
. . .

*Choose the meatiest spare ribs you can find, to make these a real success, and
remember to keep a supply of paper napkins within easy reach.*

2 Mix together all the remaining
ingredients, except the spring onions,
and pour over the ribs. Toss well to
coat evenly. Cover the bowl and leave
to marinate in the fridge overnight.

3 Cook the ribs on a medium-hot
barbecue, turning frequently, for about
30–40 minutes. Brush occasionally
with the remaining marinade.

INGREDIENTS

*1kg/2¼lb Chinese-style pork
spare ribs
10ml/2 tsp Chinese five-spice
powder
2 garlic cloves, crushed
15ml/1 tbsp grated fresh
root ginger
2.5ml/½ tsp chilli sauce
60ml/4 tbsp dark soy sauce
45ml/3 tbsp dark muscovado sugar
15ml/1 tbsp sunflower oil
4 spring onions*

SERVES 4

1 If the spare ribs are still attached
to each other, cut between them to
separate them (or you could ask your
butcher to do this when you buy them).
Place the spare ribs in a large bowl.

4 While the ribs are cooking, finely
slice the spring onions. Scatter them
over the ribs and serve immediately.

SALMON WITH SPICY PESTO

• • •

*This is a great way to bone salmon steaks to give a solid piece of fish. The pesto uses
sunflower kernels and chilli as its flavouring, rather than the classic basil and pine nuts.*

INGREDIENTS

*4 salmon steaks, about
225g/8oz each
30ml/2 tbsp sunflower oil
finely grated rind and juice
of 1 lime
salt and freshly ground
black pepper*

FOR THE PESTO
*6 mild fresh red chillies
2 garlic cloves
30ml/2 tbsp sunflower or
pumpkin seeds
juice and finely grated rind
of 1 lime
75ml/5 tbsp olive oil*

SERVES 4

1 Insert a very sharp knife close to
the top of the bone. Working closely
to the bone, cut your way to the end
of the steak to release one side. Repeat
with the other side. Pull out any extra
visible bones with a pair of tweezers.

2 Sprinkle salt on the work surface
and take hold of the end of the salmon
piece, skin-side down. Insert the knife
between the skin and the flesh and,
working away from you, remove the
skin, keeping the knife as close to it as
possible. Repeat for each piece of fish.

3 Curl each piece of fish into a
round, with the thinner end wrapped
around the fatter end. Secure the shape
tightly with a length of string.

4 Rub the sunflower oil into the
boneless fish rounds. Put the salmon
into a large bowl or dish and add the
lime juice and rind and the salt and
pepper. Allow the salmon to marinate
in the fridge for up to 2 hours.

5 For the pesto, de-seed the chillies
and place with the garlic cloves,
sunflower or pumpkin seeds, lime juice,
rind and seasoning in a food processor.
Process until well mixed. Pour the olive
oil gradually over the moving blades
until the sauce has thickened and
emulsified. Drain the salmon from its
marinade. Cook the fish steaks on a
medium barbecue for 5 minutes each
side and serve with the spicy pesto.

GRILLED KING PRAWNS WITH ROMESCO SAUCE

· · ·

This sauce comes from the Catalan region of Spain and is served with fish and seafood.
Its main ingredients are sweet pepper, tomatoes, garlic and almonds.

INGREDIENTS

24 uncooked king prawns
30–45ml/2–3 tbsp olive oil
flat leaf parsley, to garnish
lemon wedges, to serve

FOR THE SAUCE
2 well-flavoured tomatoes
60ml/4 tbsp olive oil
1 onion, chopped
4 garlic cloves, chopped
1 canned pimiento, chopped
2.5ml/½ tsp dried chilli flakes or powder
75ml/5 tbsp fish stock
30ml/2 tbsp white wine
10 blanched almonds
15ml/1 tbsp red wine vinegar
salt

SERVES 4

1 To make the sauce, immerse the tomatoes in boiling water for about 30 seconds, then refresh them under cold running water. Peel away the skins and roughly chop the flesh.

2 Heat 30ml/2 tbsp of the oil. Add the onion and three of the garlic cloves and cook until soft. Add the pimiento, tomatoes, chilli, fish stock and wine. Cover and simmer for 30 minutes.

3 Toast the almonds under the grill until golden. Transfer to a blender or food processor and grind coarsely. Add the remaining 30ml/2 tbsp of oil, the vinegar and the last garlic clove and process until evenly combined. Add the tomato and pimiento sauce and process until smooth. Season with salt.

4 Remove the heads from the prawns, leaving them otherwise unshelled and, with a sharp knife, slit each one down the back and remove the dark vein. Rinse and pat dry on kitchen paper. Toss the prawns in olive oil, then spread them out on the barbecue and cook over a medium heat for about 2–3 minutes on each side, until pink. Serve at once, garnished with parsley and accompanied by lemon wedges and the romesco sauce.

GRILLED MUSSELS WITH PARSLEY AND PARMESAN

• • •

Mussels release an irresistible aroma as they cook on the barbecue: don't be surprised
if they are devoured the moment they are ready.

INGREDIENTS

450g/1lb fresh mussels
45ml/3 tbsp water
15ml/1 tbsp melted butter
15ml/1 tbsp olive oil
45ml/3 tbsp freshly grated
Parmesan cheese
30ml/2 tbsp chopped fresh parsley
2 garlic cloves, finely chopped
2.5ml/½ tsp coarsely ground black
pepper

SERVES 4

2 Place the mussels with the water in a large saucepan. Cover with the lid and steam for 5 minutes, or until all of the mussels have opened.

4 In a large bowl, mix together the melted butter, olive oil, grated Parmesan cheese, chopped parsley, garlic and ground black pepper.

1 Scrub the mussels, scraping off any barnacles and pulling out the beards. Tap any closed mussels sharply with a knife and discard any that fail to open.

3 Drain the mussels, discarding any that remain closed. Snap the top shell off each, leaving the mussel still attached to the bottom shell.

5 Using a spoon, place a small amount of the cheese mixture on top of each mussel.

6 Cook the mussels in a saucepan on a medium barbecue for 2–3 minutes or until the mussels are sizzling hot. Serve immediately, with crusty French bread.

QUICK SEAFOOD PIZZA
∘ ∘ ∘

Make four mini pizzas or one large one with the same quantities of ingredients.
If you are short of time, use a pizza-base mix instead of making the dough.

INGREDIENTS

FOR THE PIZZA BASE
5ml/1 tsp easy-blend yeast
450g/1lb/4 cups strong bread flour
15ml/1tbsp sugar
5ml/1tsp sea salt
300ml/½ pint/1¼ cups
lukewarm water
30ml/2tbsp extra virgin olive oil

FOR THE FISH TOPPING
15ml/1 tbsp olive oil
1 onion, finely chopped
800g/1¾ lb canned or fresh plum
tomatoes, chopped
salt and freshly ground black
pepper
15ml/1 tbsp chopped fresh thyme
100g/4oz cherry tomatoes, halved
12 fresh anchovy fillets, or 1 can
anchovy fillets, drained
8 fresh, peeled prawns
a few sprigs of fresh thyme,
to garnish

SERVES 4

1 Stir the easy-blend yeast into the flour in a large bowl. Add the sugar and sea salt and mix together well.

2 Add the water and olive oil to the bowl, and stir to make a firm dough.

3 Knead the dough for about 10 minutes. Cover and leave in a warm place until it has doubled in size.

4 Knock back the dough and knead for 5 minutes, then cut the dough into four. Shape each of the four pieces of dough into 13m/5in circles.

5 Fry the onions until soft. Add the canned tomatoes, seasoning and thyme and simmer for 15 minutes. Brush the pizza bases with olive oil and cook on a medium-hot barbecue, oiled side down, for about 6–8 minutes, until firm and golden underneath. Oil the uncooked side and turn the pizzas over.

6 Cut the cherry tomatoes in half. Assemble each of the pizzas with a spoonful of the sauce, a couple of anchovy fillets and prawns and the cherry tomatoes. Return the pizzas to the barbecue and cook for a further 8–10 minutes until golden and crispy. Scatter a few fresh sprigs of thyme on top of the pizzas to serve.

Variation
Add your favourite seafood, such as fresh or canned mussels, to the topping.

CIABATTA WITH MOZZARELLA AND ONIONS
• • •

*Ciabatta bread is readily available and is even more delicious when made with spinach,
sun-dried tomatoes or olives: you can find these variations in most supermarkets.*

INGREDIENTS

*1 ciabatta loaf
60ml/4 tbsp red pesto
2 small onions
olive oil, for brushing
225g/8oz mozzarella cheese, sliced
8 black olives, halved and stoned*

MAKES 4

1 Cut the bread in half horizontally
and toast the cut sides lightly on the
barbecue. Spread with the red pesto.

2 Peel the onions and cut them
horizontally into slices. Brush with oil
and cook on a hot barbecue for 4–5
minutes until the edges are caramelized.

3 Arrange the cheese slices on the
bread. Add the onion slices and scatter
some olives over. Cut in half. Return to
the barbecue or grill to melt the cheese.

40

CROSTINI WITH TOMATO AND ANCHOVY

• • •

Crostini are little rounds of bread cut from a baguette and crisply toasted, then covered with a topping such as this savoury mixture of tomato and anchovy.

2 Cut the bread diagonally into 8 slices about 1cm/½in thick and brush with the remaining oil. Toast on the barbecue until golden, turning once.

3 Spoon a little tomato mixture on to each slice of bread. Place an anchovy fillet on each one and dot with the halved olives. Serve the crostini garnished with a sprig of fresh basil.

INGREDIENTS

60ml/4 tbsp olive oil
2 garlic cloves
4 tomatoes, peeled and chopped
15ml/1 tbsp chopped fresh basil
15ml/1 tbsp tomato paste
1 small baguette (large enough to give 8 slices)
8 canned anchovy fillets
12 black olives, halved and stoned
salt and freshly ground black pepper
fresh basil, to garnish

MAKES 8

1 Heat half the olive oil in a frying pan and fry the whole garlic cloves with the chopped tomatoes for about 4 minutes. Stir in the chopped basil, tomato paste and season with plenty of salt and freshly ground black pepper.

Variation

CROSTINI WITH ONION AND OLIVE
Fry 2 large onions, sliced, in 30ml/2 tbsp olive oil until golden. Stir in 8 chopped anchovy fillets, 12 halved, stoned black olives, some seasoning, and 5ml/1 tsp dried thyme. Spread the bread with 15ml/1 tbsp black olive paste and cover with the onion mixture.

41

MEAT DISHES

———◆———

Succulent grilled cuts of meat are often the starting-point when planning

a meal cooked on the barbecue, and char-grilling gives meat a unique

flavour. A perfect steak or lamb chop, simply seasoned and brushed with

oil before grilling, is utterly delicious. Even ordinary sausages and

burgers for an impromptu family supper can be turned into a treat on

the barbecue. But with a little forethought you can add variety and

originality to your cooking by marinating the meat for a few hours

before you cook it. The simplest marinade will work wonders:

improving the texture and juiciness of the meat as well as adding

the flavours of herbs and spices. The recipes in this chapter draw on

cuisines from all over the world to offer an exciting range of dishes

that are all easy to prepare and delicious.

MIXED GRILL SKEWERS WITH HORSERADISH SAUCE

This hearty selection of meats, cooked on a skewer and drizzled with horseradish sauce, makes a popular main course. Keep all the pieces of meat about the same thickness so they cook evenly.

INGREDIENTS

4 small lamb noisettes, each about 2.5cm/1in thick
4 lamb's kidneys
4 streaky bacon rashers
8 cherry tomatoes
8 chipolata sausages
12–16 bay leaves
salt and freshly ground black pepper

FOR THE HORSERADISH SAUCE
30ml/2 tbsp horseradish relish
45ml/3 tbsp melted butter

SERVES 4

1 Trim any excess fat from the lamb noisettes with a sharp knife. Halve the kidneys and remove the cores, using kitchen scissors.

2 Cut each bacon rasher in half and wrap around the tomatoes or kidneys.

3 Thread the lamb noissettes, bacon-wrapped kidneys and cherry tomatoes, chipolatas and bay leaves on to four long metal skewers. Set aside while you prepare the sauce.

4 Mix the horseradish relish with the melted butter in a small bowl and stir until thoroughly mixed.

5 Brush a little of the horseradish sauce over the meat and sprinkle with salt and freshly ground black pepper.

6 Cook the skewers on a medium barbecue for 12 minutes, turning occasionally, until the meat is golden brown and thoroughly cooked. Serve hot, drizzled with the remaining sauce.

SAUSAGES WITH PRUNES AND BACON

. . .

Sausages are a perennial barbecue favourite and this is a delicious way to ring the changes.
Serve with crusty French bread or warmed ciabatta.

2 Spread the cut surface with the mustard and then place three prunes in each sausage, pressing them in firmly.

3 Stretch the bacon rashers out thinly, using the back of a palette knife.

4 Wrap one bacon rasher tightly around each of the sausages, to hold them in shape. Cook over a hot barbecue for 15–18 minutes, turning occasionally, until evenly browned and thoroughly cooked. Serve at once, with lots of fresh crusty bread and the additional mustard.

INGREDIENTS

8 large, meaty sausages, such as
Toulouse or other good-quality
pork sausages
30ml/2 tbsp Dijon mustard, plus
extra to serve
24 ready-to-eat prunes
8 smoked streaky
bacon rashers

SERVES 4

1 Use a sharp knife to cut a long slit down the length of each sausage, about three-quarters of the way through.

SHISH KEBAB

° ° °

Many different kinds of kebab are eaten throughout the Middle East, and they are almost always cooked over an open wood or charcoal fire.

INGREDIENTS

450g/1lb boned leg of lamb, cubed
1 large green pepper, seeded and
cut into squares
1 large yellow pepper, seeded and
cut into squares
8 baby onions, halved
225g/8oz button mushrooms
4 tomatoes, halved
15ml/1 tbsp melted butter
bulgur wheat, to serve

FOR THE MARINADE
45ml/3 tbsp olive oil
juice of 1 lemon
2 garlic cloves, crushed
1 large onion, grated
15ml/1 tbsp fresh oregano
salt and freshly ground black
pepper

SERVES 4

1 First make the marinade: blend together the olive oil, lemon juice, crushed garlic, onion, fresh oregano and seasoning. Place the meat in a shallow dish and pour over the marinade. Cover with clear film and leave to marinate for several hours, or overnight, in the fridge.

2 Thread the lamb on to metal skewers, alternating with pieces of pepper, onions and mushrooms. Thread the tomatoes on to separate skewers.

3 Cook the kebabs and tomatoes on a hot barbecue for 10 minutes, turning occasionally and basting with butter. Serve with bulgur wheat.

BACON KOFTA KEBABS AND SALAD

• • •

*Kofta kebabs can be made with any type of minced meat, but bacon is very successful,
if you have a food processor.*

INGREDIENTS

250g/9oz lean streaky bacon
rashers, roughly chopped
1 small onion, roughly chopped
1 celery stick, roughly chopped
75ml/5 tbsp fresh wholemeal
breadcrumbs
45ml/3 tbsp chopped fresh thyme
30ml/2 tbsp Worcestershire sauce
1 egg, beaten
salt and freshly ground black
pepper
olive oil, for brushing

FOR THE SALAD

115g/4oz/³/₄ cup bulgur wheat
60ml/4 tbsp toasted sunflower
seeds
15ml/1 tbsp olive oil
salt and freshly ground black
pepper
handful celery leaves, chopped

SERVES 4

1 Place the bacon, onion, celery and breadcrumbs in a food processor and process until chopped. Add the thyme, Worcestershire sauce and seasoning. Bind to a firm mixture with the egg.

2 Divide the mixture into eight equal portions and use your hands to shape them around eight bamboo skewers.

3 For the salad, place the bulgur wheat in a bowl and pour over boiling water to cover. Leave to stand for 30 minutes, until the grains are tender.

4 Drain well, then stir in the sunflower seeds, olive oil, salt and pepper. Stir in the celery leaves.

5 Cook the kofta skewers over a medium-hot barbecue for 8–10 minutes, turning occasionally, until golden brown. Serve with the salad.

PEPPERED STEAKS IN BEER AND GARLIC

The robust flavours of this dish will satisfy the heartiest appetites.
Serve the steaks with jacket potatoes and a crisp mixed salad.

2 Remove the steaks from the dish and reserve the marinade. Sprinkle the peppercorns over the steaks and press them into the surface.

3 Cook the steaks on a hot barbecue, basting them occasionally with the reserved marinade during cooking. (Take care when basting, as the alcohol will tend to flare up: spoon or brush on just a small amount at a time.)

INGREDIENTS

4 beef sirloin or rump steaks,
about 175g/6oz each
2 garlic cloves, crushed
120ml/4fl oz/¹/₂ cup brown
ale or stout
30ml/2 tbsp dark muscovado sugar
30ml/2 tbsp Worcestershire sauce
15ml/1 tbsp corn oil
15ml/1 tbsp crushed black
peppercorns

SERVES 4

1 Place the steaks in a dish and add the garlic, ale or stout, sugar, Worcestershire sauce and oil. Turn to coat evenly, then leave to marinate in the fridge for 2–3 hours or overnight.

4 Turn the steaks once during cooking, and cook them for about 3–6 minutes on each side, depending on how rare you like them.

SIRLOIN STEAKS WITH BLOODY MARY SAUCE
∘ ∘ ∘

This cocktail of ingredients is just as delicious as the drink that inspired it, and as the alcohol evaporates in cooking you need not worry about a hangover.

INGREDIENTS

4 sirloin steaks, about 225g/8oz each

FOR THE MARINADE
30ml/2 tbsp dark soy sauce
60ml/4 tbsp balsamic vinegar
30ml/2 tbsp olive oil

FOR THE BLOODY MARY SAUCE
1kg/2¼lb very ripe tomatoes, peeled and chopped
tomato purée, if required
50g/2oz/½ cup chopped onions
2 spring onions
5ml/1 tsp chopped fresh coriander
5ml/1 tsp ground cumin
5ml/1 tsp salt
15ml/1 tbsp fresh lime juice
120ml/4fl oz/½ cup beef consommé
60ml/4 tbsp vodka
15ml/1 tbsp Worcestershire sauce

SERVES 4

1 Lay the steaks in a shallow dish. Mix the marinade ingredients together, pour over the steaks and leave to marinate in the fridge for at least 2 hours, turning once or twice.

2 Place all the sauce ingredients in a food processor and blend to a fairly smooth texture. If the tomatoes are not quite ripe, add a little tomato purée. Put in a saucepan, bring to the boil and simmer for about 5 minutes.

3 Remove the steaks from the dish and discard the marinade. Cook the steaks on a medium-hot barbecue for about 3–6 minutes each side, depending on how rare you like them, turning once during cooking. Serve the steaks with the Bloody Mary sauce.

BEEF RIB WITH ONION SAUCE

• • •

Rib of beef is a classic large roasting joint, but just one rib, barbecued on the bone then carved into succulent slices, makes a perfect dish for two. Serve with a mellow red onion sauce.

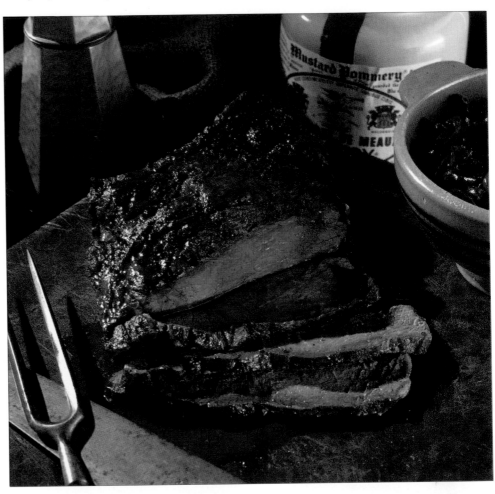

INGREDIENTS

1 beef rib on the bone, about
1kg/2¼lb and about 4cm/1½ in
thick, well trimmed of fat
5ml/1 tsp "steak pepper" or lightly
crushed black peppercorns
15ml/1 tbsp coarse sea salt,
crushed
30–45ml/2–3 tbsp olive oil

FOR THE RED ONION SAUCE
40g/1½ oz butter
1 large red onion or 8–10 shallots,
sliced
250ml/8fl oz/1 cup fruity red wine
250ml/8fl oz/1 cup beef or chicken
stock
15–30ml/1–2 tbsp redcurrant jelly
or seedless raspberry preserve
1.5ml/¼ tsp dried thyme
salt and freshly ground black
pepper

SERVES 2

1 Wipe the beef with damp kitchen paper. Mix the "steak pepper" or crushed peppercorns with the crushed salt and press on to both sides of the meat. Leave the meat to stand, loosely covered, for 30 minutes.

2 To make the sauce, melt the butter over a medium heat. Add the onion or shallots and cook for 3 minutes until softened. Add the wine, stock, jelly or preserve and thyme and bring to the boil. Reduce the heat and simmer for 30–35 minutes until the liquid has evaporated and the sauce has thickened. Season and keep warm.

3 Brush the meat with olive oil and cook on a hot barbecue, or in a pan over a high heat, for 5–8 minutes each side, depending on how rare you like it. Transfer the beef to a board, cover loosely and leave to stand for about 10 minutes. Using a knife, loosen the meat from the rib bone, then carve into thick slices. Serve with the red onion sauce.

STILTON BURGERS

*A variation on the traditional burger, this tasty recipe contains a delicious surprise:
a creamy filling of lightly melted Stilton cheese.*

INGREDIENTS

*450g/1lb/4 cups minced beef
1 onion, chopped
1 celery stick, chopped
5ml/1 tsp dried mixed herbs
5ml/1 tsp prepared mustard
50g/2oz/¹⁄₂ cup crumbled Stilton
cheese
4 burger buns
salt and freshly ground black
pepper*

SERVES 4

1 Mix the minced beef with the chopped onion, celery, mixed herbs and mustard. Season well with salt and pepper, and bring together with your hands to form a firm mixture.

2 Divide the mixture into eight equal portions. Shape four portions into rounds and flatten each one slightly. Place a little of the crumbled cheese in the centre of each round.

3 Shape and flatten the remaining four portions and place on top. Use your hands to mould the rounds together, encasing the crumbled cheese, and shaping them into four burgers.

4 Cook on a medium barbecue for about 10 minutes or until cooked through, turning once. Split the burger buns and place a burger inside each. Serve with salad and mustard pickle.

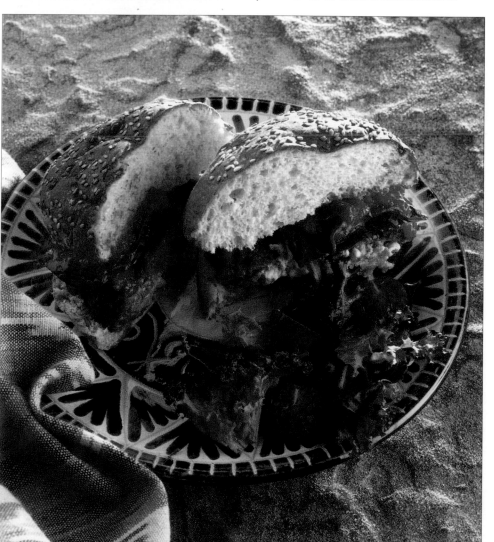

53

THAI BEEF SALAD

. . .

A hearty salad of beef and crunchy vegetables, laced with a tangy chilli and lime dressing.
The barbecued meat gives a truly delicious flavour to the salad.

INGREDIENTS

2 sirloin steaks, about
225g/8oz each
1 red onion, finely sliced
½ cucumber, finely sliced into
matchsticks
1 stalk lemon grass, finely chopped
30ml/2 tbsp chopped spring onions
juice of 2 limes
15–30ml/1–2 tbsp Thai fish sauce
2–4 red chillies, finely sliced, to
garnish
fresh coriander, Chinese mustard
cress and mint leaves, to garnish

SERVES 4

1 Barbecue or pan-fry the beef steaks until they are medium-rare. Allow the steaks to rest for 10–15 minutes.

2 When the steaks have cooled slightly, slice them thinly, using a heavy knife, and put the slices into a large bowl.

3 Add the sliced onion, cucumber matchsticks and chopped lemon grass.

4 Add the spring onions. Toss and season with lime juice and Thai fish sauce. Serve at room temperature or chilled, garnished with the chillies, coriander, mustard cress and mint.

NEW ORLEANS STEAK SALAD

* * *

The New Orleans "Poor Boy" started life in the Italian Creole community, as a sandwich filled with leftover scraps. This salad, made with tender beef steak, is a variation on the sandwich.

INGREDIENTS

4 sirloin or rump steaks,
about 175g/6oz each
1 escarole lettuce
1 bunch watercress
4 tomatoes, quartered
4 large gherkins, sliced
4 spring onions, sliced
4 canned artichoke hearts, halved
175g/6oz button mushrooms,
sliced
12 green olives
120ml/4fl oz French dressing
salt and freshly ground black
pepper

SERVES 4

1 Season the steaks with plenty of black pepper and cook on a hot barbecue, or under a hot grill, for 4–6 minutes, turning once, until medium-rare. Cover and leave the steaks to rest in a warm place.

2 Combine the salad leaves with all the ingredients except the steak, and toss with the French dressing.

3 Divide the salad between 4 plates. Slice each steak diagonally and arrange the slices over the salad. Season with salt and fresh black pepper and serve.

SPICED BEEF SATAY

∘ ∘ ∘

Tender strips of steak threaded on skewers and spiced with the characteristic flavours of Indonesia are popular with everyone.

INGREDIENTS
*450g/1lb rump steak, cut in
1cm/¹/₂ in strips
5ml/1 tsp coriander seeds, dry-fried
and ground
2.5ml/¹/₂ tsp cumin seeds, dry-fried
and ground
5ml/1 tsp tamarind pulp
1 small onion
2 garlic cloves
15ml/1 tbsp brown sugar
15ml/1 tbsp dark soy sauce
salt*

TO SERVE
*cucumber chunks
lemon or lime wedges
Sambal Kecap*

MAKES 18 SKEWERS

1 Mix the meat and spices in a large non-metallic bowl. Soak the tamarind pulp in 75ml/3fl oz/¹/₃ cup water.

2 Strain the tamarind and reserve the juice. Put the onion, garlic, tamarind juice, sugar and soy sauce in a food processor and blend well.

3 Pour the marinade over the meat and spices in the bowl and toss well together. Leave for at least 1 hour.

4 Meanwhile, soak some bamboo skewers in water to prevent them from burning while cooking. Thread 5 or 6 pieces of meat on to each skewer and sprinkle with salt. Cook on a medium-hot barbecue, turning the skewers frequently and basting with the marinade, until the meat is tender.

5 Serve with cucumber chunks and wedges of lemon or lime for squeezing over the meat. Sambal Kecap makes a traditional accompaniment.

SAMBAL KECAP
Mix 1 fresh red chilli, seeded and finely chopped, 2 crushed garlic cloves and 60ml/4 tbsp dark soy sauce with 20ml/4 tsp lemon juice and 30ml/2 tbsp hot water in a bowl. Leave to stand for 30 minutes before serving.

VEGETABLE-STUFFED BEEF ROLLS
. . .

*These Japanese-style beef rolls are very popular for al fresco meals. You could roll up many
other vegetables in the sliced beef. Pork is also very good cooked this way.*

INGREDIENTS

50g/2oz carrot
50g/2oz green pepper, seeded
bunch of spring onions
400g/14oz beef topside,
thinly sliced
plain flour, for dusting
15ml/1 tbsp olive oil
fresh parsley sprigs, to garnish

FOR THE SAUCE
30ml/2 tbsp sugar
45ml/3 tbsp soy sauce
45ml/3 tbsp mirin

SERVES 4

1 Use a sharp knife to shred the carrot and green pepper into 4–5cm/1½–2in lengths. Wash and peel the outer skins from the spring onions, then halve them lengthways. Shred the spring onions diagonally into 4–5cm/1½–2in lengths.

2 The beef slices should be no more than 2mm/1/12 in thick, and about 15cm/6in square. Lay a slice of beef on a chopping board and top with strips of the carrot, green pepper and spring onion. Roll up quite tightly and dust lightly with flour. Repeat with the remaining beef and vegetables.

3 Secure the beef rolls with cocktail sticks, soaked in water to prevent them from burning, and cook on a medium barbecue or in a pan over a medium heat, for 10–15 minutes, turning frequently, until golden brown and thoroughly cooked.

4 Blend the ingredients for the sauce in a small pan and cook to dissolve the sugar and form a glaze. Halve the cooked rolls, cutting at a slant, and stand them on a plate with the sloping cut ends facing upwards. Dress with the sauce and garnish with fresh parsley.

LAMB STEAKS MARINATED IN MINT AND SHERRY

• • •

*The marinade in this recipe is extremely quick to prepare, and is the key
to its success: the sherry imparts a wonderful tang to the meat.*

INGREDIENTS
6 large lamb steaks or
12 smaller chops

FOR THE MARINADE
30ml/2 tbsp chopped fresh mint
leaves
15ml/1 tbsp black peppercorns
1 medium onion, chopped
120ml/4fl oz/½ cup sherry
60ml/4 tbsp extra virgin olive oil
2 garlic cloves

SERVES 6

1 Blend the mint leaves and
peppercorns in a food processor until
finely chopped. Add the onion and
process again until smooth. Add the
rest of the marinade ingredients and
process until completely mixed. The
marinade should be a thick consistency.

2 Add the marinade to the steaks or
chops and cover with clear film. Leave
in the fridge to marinate overnight.

3 Cook the steaks on a medium
barbecue for 10–15 minutes, basting
occasionally with the marinade.

SKEWERED LAMB WITH CORIANDER YOGURT
° ° ∘

These Turkish kebabs are traditionally made with lamb, but lean beef or pork work equally well.
You can alternate pieces of pepper, lemon or onions with the meat for extra flavour and colour.

INGREDIENTS

900g/2lb lean boneless lamb
1 large onion, grated
3 bay leaves
5 thyme or rosemary sprigs
grated rind and juice of 1 lemon
2.5ml/½ tsp caster sugar
75ml/3fl oz/⅓ cup olive oil
salt and freshly ground black pepper
sprigs of fresh rosemary, to garnish
barbecued lemon wedges, to serve

FOR THE CORIANDER YOGURT
150ml/¼ pint/⅔ cup thick natural yogurt
15ml/1 tbsp chopped fresh mint
15ml/1 tbsp chopped fresh coriander
10ml/2 tsp grated onion

SERVES 4

1 To make the coriander yogurt, mix together the natural yogurt, chopped fresh mint, chopped fresh coriander and grated onion. Transfer the yogurt to a serving bowl.

2 To make the kebabs, cut the lamb into 2.5cm/1in cubes and put in a bowl. Mix together the onion, herbs, lemon rind and juice, sugar and oil, then season to taste.

3 Pour the marinade over the meat in the bowl and stir to ensure the meat is thoroughly covered. Cover with clear film and leave to marinate in the fridge for several hours or overnight.

4 Drain the meat and thread on to metal skewers. Cook on a hot barbecue for about 10 minutes. Garnish with rosemary and barbecued lemon wedges and serve with the coriander yogurt.

LAMB BURGERS WITH REDCURRANT CHUTNEY

*These rather special burgers take a little extra time to prepare but are well worth it.
The redcurrant chutney is the perfect complement to the minty lamb taste.*

INGREDIENTS

500g/1¼ lb minced lean lamb
1 small onion, finely chopped
30ml/2 tbsp finely chopped
fresh mint
30ml/2 tbsp finely chopped
fresh parsley
115g/4oz mozzarella cheese
30ml/2 tbsp oil, for basting
salt and freshly ground black
pepper

FOR THE REDCURRANT CHUTNEY
115g/4oz/1½ cups fresh or frozen
redcurrants
10ml/2 tsp clear honey
5ml/1 tsp balsamic vinegar
30ml/2 tbsp finely chopped mint

SERVES 4

1 In a large bowl, mix together the minced lamb, chopped onion, mint and parsley until evenly combined. Season well with plenty of salt and freshly ground black pepper.

Cook's Tip

If time is short, or if fresh redcurrants are not available, serve the burgers with ready-made redcurrant sauce.

2 Roughly divide the meat mixture into eight equal pieces and use your hands to press each of the pieces into flat rounds.

3 Cut the mozzarella cheese into four chunks. Place one chunk of cheese on half the lamb rounds. Top each with another round of meat mixture.

4 Press each of the two rounds of meat together firmly, making four flattish burger shapes. Use your fingers to blend the edges and seal in the cheese completely.

5 Place all the ingredients for the chutney in a bowl and mash them together with a fork. Season well with salt and freshly ground black pepper.

6 Brush the lamb burgers with olive oil and cook them over a moderately hot barbecue for about 15 minutes, turning once, until golden brown. Serve with the redcurrant chutney.

BARBECUED LAMB WITH POTATO SLICES

° ° °

A traditional mixture of fresh herbs adds a summery flavour to this simple lamb dish.
A leg of lamb is easier to cook evenly on the barbecue if it's boned out, or "butterflied" first.

INGREDIENTS

1 leg of lamb, about 1.75kg/4½ lb
1 garlic clove, thinly sliced
handful of fresh flat-leaf parsley
handful of fresh sage
handful of fresh rosemary
handful of fresh thyme
90ml/6 tbsp dry sherry
60ml/4 tbsp walnut oil
500g/1¼ lb medium-size potatoes
salt and freshly ground
black pepper

SERVES 4

2 Use a sharp kitchen knife to scrape away the meat from the bone on both sides, until the bone is completely exposed. Carefully remove the bone and cut away any sinews and excess fat from the meat.

4 Place the meat in a bowl and pour over the sherry and walnut oil. Chop half the remaining herbs and scatter over the meat. Cover the bowl with a clean dish towel and leave to marinate in the fridge for 30 minutes.

1 Place the lamb on a board, smooth side downwards, so that you can see where the bone lies. Using a sharp heavy knife, make a long cut through the flesh down to the bone.

3 Cut through the thickest part of the meat so that you can open it out as flat as possible. Make several cuts in the lamb with a sharp kitchen knife, and push slivers of garlic and sprigs of fresh herbs into the cuts.

5 Remove the lamb from the marinade and season. Cook on a medium-hot barbecue for 30–35 minutes, turning occasionally and basting with the reserved marinade.

Cook's Tip

If you have a spit-roasting attachment, the lamb can be rolled and tied with herbs inside, and spit roasted for 1–1½ hours. A spit makes it much easier to cook larger pieces of lamb.

6 Scrub the potatoes, then cut them in thick slices. Brush with the marinade and place around the lamb. Cook for about 15 minutes, until golden brown.

LAMB WITH LAVENDER BALSAMIC MARINADE
. . .

Lavender is an unusual flavour to use with meat, but its heady, summery scent works well with barbecued lamb. If you prefer, rosemary can take its place.

2 Sprinkle the chopped fresh lavender over the lamb in the bowl.

3 Beat together the vinegar, olive oil and lemon juice and pour them over the lamb. Season well with salt and pepper and then turn to coat evenly.

4 Scatter a few lavender sprigs over the grill or on the coals of a medium-hot barbecue. Cook the lamb for about 15–20 minutes, turning once and basting with any remaining marinade, until golden brown on the outside and still slightly pink in the centre.

INGREDIENTS
4 racks of lamb, with 3–4 cutlets each
1 shallot, finely chopped
45ml/3 tbsp chopped fresh lavender
15ml/1 tbsp balsamic vinegar
30ml/2 tbsp olive oil
15ml/1 tbsp lemon juice
salt and freshly ground black pepper
handful of lavender sprigs

SERVES 4

1 Place the racks of lamb in a large mixing bowl or wide dish and sprinkle over the chopped shallot.

LAMB WITH MINT AND LEMON
. . .

Use this simple and traditional marinade to make the most of fine quality lamb leg steaks.
Lemon and fresh mint combine extremely well with the flavour of barbecued lamb.

INGREDIENTS
4 lamb steaks, about
225g/8oz each
fresh mint leaves, to garnish

FOR THE MARINADE
grated rind and juice of ½ lemon
1 garlic clove, crushed
1 spring onion, finely chopped
5ml/1 tsp finely chopped fresh mint
30ml/2 tbsp extra virgin olive oil
salt and freshly ground black
pepper

SERVES 4

1 Mix all the marinade ingredients and season to taste. Place the lamb steaks in a shallow dish and add the marinade. Cover with clear film and leave to marinate in the fridge for several hours or overnight.

2 Drain the lamb and cook on a medium-hot barbecue for about 10–15 minutes until just cooked, basting with the marinade occasionally and turning once. Garnish the lamb steaks with the fresh mint leaves.

STUFFED AUBERGINES WITH LAMB

Minced lamb and aubergines go together beautifully. This is an attractive dish, using different coloured peppers in the lightly spiced stuffing mixture.

INGREDIENTS

2 medium aubergines
30ml/2 tbsp vegetable oil
1 medium onion, sliced
5ml/1 tsp grated fresh root ginger
5ml/1 tsp chilli powder
1 garlic clove, crushed
1.5ml/¼ tsp turmeric
5ml/1 tsp salt
5ml/1 tsp ground coriander
1 medium tomato, chopped
350g/12oz minced lean lamb
1 medium green pepper, roughly
    chopped
1 medium orange pepper, roughly
    chopped
30ml/2 tbsp chopped fresh
    coriander

FOR THE GARNISH
½ onion, sliced
2 cherry tomatoes, quartered
fresh coriander sprigs

SERVES 4

1 Cut the aubergines in half lengthways with a heavy knife. Scoop out most of the flesh and reserve it for another dish. Brush the shells with a little vegetable oil.

2 In a medium saucepan, heat 15ml/ 1 tbsp oil and fry the sliced onion until golden brown. Stir in the grated ginger, chilli powder, garlic, turmeric, salt and ground coriander. Add the chopped tomato, lower the heat and cook for about 5 minutes, stirring continuously.

3 Add the minced lamb to the saucepan and continue to cook over a medium heat for about 7–10 minutes. Stir in the chopped fresh peppers and the fresh coriander.

4 Spoon the lamb mixture into the aubergine shells and brush the edges of the shells with the remaining oil. Cook on a medium barbecue for 15–20 minutes until cooked through. Garnish with sliced onion, cherry tomatoes and coriander, and serve with rice, if liked.

VEAL CHOPS WITH BASIL BUTTER

∘ ∘ ∘

Veal chops from the loin are an expensive cut and are best cooked quickly and simply.
The flavour of basil goes well with veal, but other herbs can be used instead if you prefer.

INGREDIENTS
25g/1oz/2 tbsp butter, softened
15ml/1 tbsp Dijon mustard
15ml/1 tbsp chopped fresh basil
olive oil, for brushing
2 veal loin chops, 2.5cm/1in thick,
about 225g/8oz each
salt and freshly ground black
pepper
fresh basil sprigs, to garnish

SERVES 2

1 To make the basil butter, cream the softened butter with the Dijon mustard and chopped fresh basil in a large mixing bowl, then season with plenty of freshly ground black pepper.

2 Brush both sides of each chop with olive oil and season with a little salt.

3 Cook the chops on a hot barbecue for 7–10 minutes, basting with oil and turning once, until done to your liking. (Medium-rare meat will still be slightly soft when pressed, medium meat will be springy and well-done firm.) Top each chop with half the basil butter and serve at once, garnished with basil.

PORK AND PINEAPPLE SATAY

° ° °

This variation on the classic satay has added pineapple, but keeps the traditional coconut and peanut sauce.

INGREDIENTS

500g/1¼ lb pork fillet
1 small onion, chopped
1 garlic clove, chopped
60ml/4 tbsp soy sauce
finely grated rind of ½ lemon
5ml/1 tsp ground cumin
5ml/1 tsp ground coriander
5ml/1 tsp ground turmeric
5ml/1 tsp dark muscovado sugar
225g/8oz can pineapple chunks, or
1 small fresh pineapple, peeled and diced
salt and freshly ground black pepper

FOR THE SATAY SAUCE
175ml/6fl oz/¾ cup coconut milk
115g/4oz/6 tbsp crunchy peanut butter
1 garlic clove, crushed
10ml/2 tsp soy sauce
5ml/1 tsp dark muscovado sugar

SERVES 4

2 Place the onion, garlic, soy sauce, lemon rind, spices and sugar in a blender or food processor. Add two pieces of pineapple and process until the mixture is almost smooth.

3 Add the paste to the pork, tossing well to coat evenly. Thread the pieces of pork on to bamboo skewers, with the remaining pineapple pieces.

4 To make the sauce, pour the coconut milk into a small saucepan and stir in the peanut butter. Stir in the remaining sauce ingredients and heat gently over the barbecue, stirring until smooth and hot. Cover and keep warm on the edge of the barbecue.

5 Cook the pork and pineapple skewers on a medium-hot barbecue for 10–12 minutes, turning occasionally, until golden brown and thoroughly cooked. Serve with the satay sauce.

1 Using a sharp kitchen knife, trim any fat from the pork fillet and cut it in 2.5cm/1in cubes. Place the meat in a large mixing bowl and set aside.

Cook's Tip
If you cannot buy coconut milk, use creamed coconut in a block. Dissolve a 50g/2oz piece in 150ml/¼ pint/⅔ cup boiling water and use as above.

LEMON GRASS PORK CHOPS WITH MUSHROOMS

* * *

Thai flavourings are used to make an aromatic marinade and a spicy sauce. The sauce can be put together in a pan on the barbecue while the chops and mushrooms are cooking.

INGREDIENTS

4 pork chops, about 225g/8oz each
4 large field mushrooms
45ml/3 tbsp vegetable oil
4 red chillies, seeded and finely sliced
45ml/3 tbsp Thai fish sauce
90ml/6 tbsp lime juice
4 shallots, chopped
5ml/1 tsp roasted ground rice
30ml/2 tbsp spring onions, chopped
fresh coriander leaves, to garnish
4 spring onions, shredded, to garnish

FOR THE MARINADE
2 garlic cloves, chopped
15ml/1 tbsp sugar
15ml/1 tbsp Thai fish sauce
30ml/2 tbsp soy sauce
15ml/1 tbsp sesame oil
15ml/1 tbsp whisky or dry sherry
2 stalks lemon grass, finely chopped
2 spring onions, chopped

SERVES 4

3 Place the mushrooms and marinated pork chops on a rack and brush with 15ml/1 tbsp vegetable oil. Cook the pork chops on a medium-hot barbecue for 10–15 minutes and the mushrooms for about 2 minutes, turning once. Brush both with the marinade while cooking.

4 Meanwhile, heat the remaining oil in a small frying pan, then remove from the heat and mix in the remaining ingredients. Put the pork chops and mushrooms on a serving plate and spoon over the sauce. Garnish with the fresh coriander leaves and shredded spring onions.

1 To make the marinade, mix all the ingredients together . Arrange the pork chops in a shallow dish. Pour over the marinade and leave for 1–2 hours.

FARMHOUSE PIZZA

. . .

Pizza is not a dish usually associated with barbecue cooking, but in fact the open fire gives the base a wonderfully crisp texture. Shape the dough to fit the grill rack of your barbecue.

INGREDIENTS

90ml/6 tbsp olive oil
225g/8oz button mushrooms,
sliced
300g/11oz packet pizza-base mix
300ml/½ pint/1¼ cups tomato
sauce
300g/11oz mozzarella cheese,
thinly sliced
115g/4oz wafer-thin smoked
ham slices
6 bottled artichoke hearts in oil,
drained and sliced
50g/2oz can anchovy fillets,
drained and halved lengthways
10 stoned black olives, halved
30ml/2 tbsp chopped fresh oregano
45ml/3 tbsp freshly grated
Parmesan cheese
freshly ground black pepper

SERVES 8

1 Heat 30ml/2 tbsp oil in a pan, add the mushrooms and fry until all the juices have evaporated. Leave to cool.

2 Make up the pizza dough according to the directions on the packet. Roll it out on a floured surface to a 30 × 25cm/12 × 10in rectangle. Brush with oil and place, oiled side down, on a medium-hot barbecue. Cook for 6 minutes until firm.

3 Brush the uncooked side of the dough with oil and turn over. Spread over the tomato sauce and arrange the sliced mozzarella on top. Scrunch up the smoked ham and arrange on top with the artichoke hearts, anchovies and cooked mushrooms.

4 Dot with the halved olives, then sprinkle over the fresh oregano and Parmesan. Drizzle over the remaining olive oil and season with black pepper. Return to the barbecue and cook for a further 8–10 minutes, or until the dough is golden brown and crisp.

POULTRY
AND GAME

——◆——

Chicken cooked on a barbecue is unfailingly popular with both adults

and children, and it can be as simple or sophisticated as you choose:

it is very versatile and takes on a whole range of flavours with great

success. Buy breast fillets to make delicious kebabs and salads with a

minimum of preparation, or cook drumsticks and thighs with robust

spicy coatings. Whole birds can be roasted very effectively on a spit,

or they can be flattened out by removing the backbone and cooked on

the grill rack. It is vital to make sure chicken is always very thoroughly

cooked – it needs a medium heat to cook it through without charring

the outside. Don't forget other types of poultry, particularly duck,

which stays beautifully juicy and moist when cooked on a barbecue.

CHICKEN WITH PINEAPPLE

• • •

The pineapple juice in this Indian recipe is used to tenderize the meat, but it also gives the chicken a deliciously tangy sweetness.

INGREDIENTS

225g/8oz can pineapple chunks
in juice
5ml/1 tsp ground cumin
5ml/1 tsp ground coriander
1 garlic clove, crushed
5ml/1 tsp chilli powder
5ml/1 tsp salt
30ml/2 tbsp natural low-fat yogurt
15ml/1 tbsp chopped fresh
coriander
few drops orange food colouring
(optional)
275g/10oz/2 cups chicken breast
and thigh meat, skinned and boned
½ red pepper
½ yellow or green pepper
1 large onion
6 cherry tomatoes
15ml/1 tbsp vegetable oil

SERVES 6

2 In a large bowl, blend together the cumin, ground coriander, garlic, chilli powder, salt, yogurt, fresh coriander and food colouring, if using. Pour in the pineapple juice and mix together.

4 Arrange the chicken pieces, vegetables and reserved pineapple chunks alternately on 6 skewers.

3 Cut the chicken into cubes, add to the yogurt and spice mixture and leave to marinate for about 1–1½ hours. Cut the peppers and onion into chunks.

5 Brush the kebabs with oil and cook on a medium barbecue for about 10 minutes, turning regularly and basting the chicken pieces regularly with the marinade, until cooked through. Serve with salad or plain boiled rice.

1 Drain the canned pineapple into a bowl. Reserve twelve large chunks of pineapple. Squeeze the juice from the remaining chunks into the bowl, then discard the chunks. You should be left with about 120ml/4fl oz/½ cup pineapple juice.

BABY CHICKENS WITH LIME AND CHILLI
. . .

Poussins are small birds which are ideal for one to two portions. The best way to prepare them is spatchcocked – flattened out – to ensure more even cooking.

INGREDIENTS
4 poussins or Cornish hens, about
450g/1lb each
45ml/3 tbsp butter
30ml/2 tbsp sun-dried tomato
paste
finely grated rind of 1 lime
10ml/2 tsp chilli sauce
juice of ½ lime
lime wedges, to serve
fresh flat leaf parsley sprigs,
to garnish

SERVES 4

2 Turn the poussin over and, with poultry shears or strong kitchen scissors, cut down either side of the backbone. Remove it and discard.

5 To hold the poussins flat during cooking, thread two bamboo skewers through each bird, crossing at the centre. Each skewer should pass through a drumstick and then out through a wing on the other side.

3 Turn the poussin breast-side up and flatten it gently. Lift the breast skin carefully and gently ease your fingertips underneath, to loosen it from the flesh.

1 Place each poussin on a chopping board, breast-side upwards, and press down firmly with your hand, to break the breastbone.

4 Mix together the butter, sun-dried tomato paste, lime rind and chilli sauce in a small bowl. Spread about three-quarters of the mixture under the skin of the poussins, smoothing it evenly over the surface of the flesh.

6 Mix the reserved paste with the lime juice and brush it over the skin of the poussins. Cook on a medium-hot barbecue, turning occasionally, for 25–30 minutes, or until there is no trace of pink in the juices when the flesh is pierced. Garnish with lime wedges and fresh flat leaf parsley.

THAI GRILLED CHICKEN

Thai grilled chicken is especially delicious when cooked on the barbecue.
Serve it on a bed of crisp salad with lime wedges to offset its richness.

INGREDIENTS

900g/2lb chicken drumsticks or
thighs
salt and freshly ground
black pepper
crisp lettuce leaves, to serve
½ cucumber, cut into strips,
to garnish
4 spring onions, trimmed,
to garnish
2 limes, quartered, to garnish

FOR THE MARINADE
5ml/1 tsp black peppercorns
2.5ml/½ tsp caraway or cumin
seeds
20ml/4 tsp sugar
10ml/2 tsp paprika
2cm/¾in piece fresh root ginger,
chopped
3 garlic cloves, crushed
15g/½oz coriander, white root or
stem, finely chopped
45ml/3 tbsp vegetable oil

SERVES 4–6

1 Chop through the narrow end of each drumstick with a heavy knife. Score the chicken pieces deeply to allow the marinade to penetrate and arrange in a shallow bowl.

2 Grind the peppercorns, caraway or cumin seeds and sugar in a pestle and mortar or a food processor. Add the paprika, ginger, garlic, coriander and oil and grind to a paste.

3 Spread the marinade over the chicken and leave to marinate in the fridge for 6 hours. Cook the chicken on a medium barbecue for about 20 minutes, basting with the marinade and turning once. Season, arrange on a bed of lettuce and garnish before serving.

MEDITERRANEAN TURKEY SKEWERS

*These attractive kebabs can be assembled in advance and left to marinate until you are ready
to cook them. Barbecuing intensifies the Mediterranean flavours of the vegetables.*

INGREDIENTS

2 medium courgettes
1 long thin aubergine
*300g/11oz boneless turkey, cut
into 5cm/2in cubes*
12–16 pickling onions
*1 red or yellow pepper, cut into
5cm/2in squares*

FOR THE MARINADE
90ml/6 tbsp olive oil
45ml/3 tbsp fresh lemon juice
1 garlic clove, finely chopped
30ml/2 tbsp chopped fresh basil
*salt and freshly ground black
pepper*

SERVES 4

3 Prepare the skewers by alternating
the turkey, onions and pepper pieces.
Lay the prepared skewers on a platter
and sprinkle with the flavoured oil.
Leave to marinate for 30 minutes.

4 Cook on a medium barbecue or
under a grill for about 10 minutes,
or until the turkey is cooked and the
vegetables are tender, turning the
skewers occasionally.

1 To make the marinade, mix the
olive oil with the lemon juice, garlic
and chopped fresh basil. Season well
with plenty of salt and black pepper.

2 Slice the courgettes and aubergine
lengthways into strips 5mm/¼ in thick.
Cut them crossways about two-thirds
down their length. Discard the shorter
lengths. Wrap half the turkey pieces
with the courgette slices and the other
half with the aubergine slices.

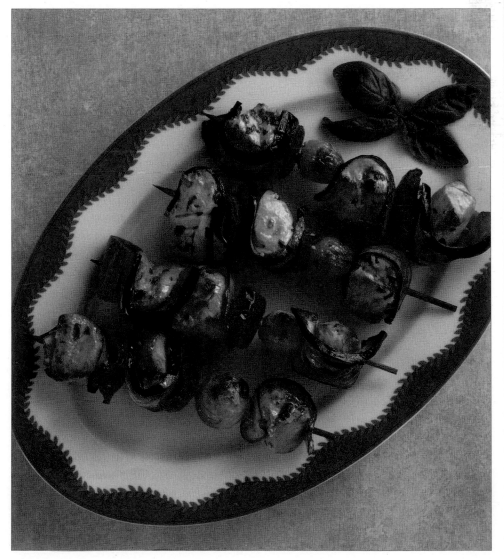

QUAIL WITH A FIVE-SPICE MARINADE

Blending and grinding your own five-spice powder for this Vietnamese dish will give the freshest-tasting results. If you are short of time, buy a ready-mixed blend from the supermarket.

INGREDIENTS

6 quails, cleaned
2 spring onions, roughly chopped, to garnish
mandarin orange or satsuma, to garnish
banana leaves, to serve

FOR THE MARINADE
2 pieces star anise
10ml/2 tsp ground cinnamon
10ml/2 tsp fennel seeds
10ml/2 tsp Sichuan pepper
a pinch ground cloves
1 small onion, finely chopped
1 garlic clove, crushed
60ml/4 tbsp clear honey
30ml/2 tbsp dark soy sauce

SERVES 4–6

1 Remove the backbones from the quails by cutting down either side with a pair of strong kitchen scissors.

2 Flatten the birds with the palm of your hand and secure each bird using two bamboo skewers.

3 To make the marinade, place the five spices in a pestle and mortar or spice mill and grind into a fine powder. Add the chopped onion, garlic, clear honey and soy sauce, and combine until thoroughly mixed.

4 Arrange the quails on a flat dish and pour over the marinade. Cover with clear film and leave in the fridge for 8 hours or overnight for the flavours to mingle.

5 Cook the quails on a medium barbecue for 15–20 minutes until golden brown, basting occasionally with the marinade and turning once.

6 To garnish, remove the outer zest from the mandarin orange or satsuma, using a vegetable peeler. Shred the zest finely and combine with the chopped spring onions. Arrange the quails on a bed of banana leaves and garnish with the orange zest and spring onions.

Cook's Tip
If you prefer, or if quails are not available, you could use other poultry such as poussins as a substitute.

PHEASANTS WITH SAGE AND LEMON
• • •

*Pheasant is quick to cook and makes a really special summer meal.
This recipe can also be used for guinea fowl.*

INGREDIENTS
2 pheasants, about 450g/1lb each
1 lemon
60ml/4 tbsp chopped fresh sage
3 shallots
5ml/1 tsp Dijon mustard
15ml/1 tbsp brandy or dry sherry
150ml/5fl oz/²⁄₃ cup crème fraîche
*salt and freshly ground black
pepper*
*lemon wedges and sage sprigs, to
garnish*

SERVES 4

2 Finely grate the rind from half the lemon and slice the rest thinly. Mix together the lemon rind and half the chopped sage in a small bowl.

3 Loosen the skin on the breasts and legs of the pheasants and push a little of the sage mixture under each. Tuck the lemon slices under the skin, smoothing the skin back firmly.

5 Meanwhile, cook the shallots on the barbecue for about 10–12 minutes, turning occasionally, until the skin is blackened and the inside very soft. Peel off the skins, chop the flesh roughly and mash it with the Dijon mustard and brandy or sherry.

6 Stir in the crème fraîche and add the reserved chopped sage. Season with plenty of salt and freshly ground black pepper. Serve the dressing with the pheasants, garnished with lemon wedges and sprigs of fresh sage.

1 Place the pheasants, breast-side upwards, on a chopping board and cut them in half lengthways, using poultry shears or a sharp kitchen knife.

4 Place the half-pheasants on a medium-hot barbecue and cook for about 25–30 minutes, turning once.

Cook's Tip
Try to choose pheasants with undamaged skins, so that the flavourings stay in place during cooking.

SPICED DUCK WITH PEARS

° . °

This delicious casserole can be cooked on the barbecue or stove. The browned pears are added towards the end of cooking, along with a pine nut and garlic paste to flavour and thicken.

INGREDIENTS

6 duck portions, either breast or
leg pieces
15ml/1 tbsp olive oil
1 large onion, thinly sliced
1 cinnamon stick, halved
2 thyme sprigs
475ml/16fl oz/2 cups duck or
chicken stock

To FINISH

3 firm ripe pears, peeled and cored
30ml/2 tbsp olive oil
2 garlic cloves, sliced
25g/1oz ⅓ cup pine nuts
2.5ml/½ tsp saffron strands
25g/1oz/2 tbsp raisins
salt and freshly ground black
pepper
thyme sprigs or parsley, to garnish

SERVES 6

1 Fry the duck portions in olive oil for 5 minutes, until golden, or brush the portions with oil and cook them on a hot barbecue for 8–10 minutes, until golden. Transfer the duck to a large flameproof dish. If frying, drain off all but 15ml/1 tbsp of fat left in the pan.

2 Fry the onion in the frying pan for 5 minutes until golden. Add the cinnamon stick, thyme and stock and bring to the boil. Pour over the duck in the dish and cook slowly on a low barbecue for about 1¼ hours.

3 Halve the pears, brush with oil and barbecue until brown, or fry the pears in the oil on the hob. Pound the garlic, pine nuts and saffron with a pestle and mortar, to make a thick, smooth paste.

4 Add the paste, raisins and pears to the flameproof dish. Cook for 15 minutes until the pears are tender.

5 Season to taste and garnish with the fresh herbs. Serve with mashed potatoes and a green vegetable, if liked.

Cook's Tip

A good stock is essential for this dish. Buy a large duck (plus two extra duck breasts if you want portions to be generous) and joint it yourself, using the giblets and carcass for stock. If you buy duck portions, use a well-flavoured chicken stock.

APRICOT DUCK WITH BEAN SPROUT SALAD

. . .

*Duck is rich in fat, so it stays beautifully moist when cooked on a barbecue,
while any excess fat drains away.*

INGREDIENTS

4 plump duck breasts, with skin
1 small red onion, thinly sliced
115g/4oz/³/4 cup ready-to-eat dried
apricots
15ml/1 tbsp clear honey
5ml/1 tsp sesame oil
10ml/2 tsp ground star anise
salt and freshly ground black
pepper

FOR THE SALAD
½ head Chinese leaves, finely
shredded
150g/5oz/2 cups bean sprouts
2 spring onions, shredded
15ml/1 tbsp light soy sauce
15ml/1 tbsp groundnut oil
5ml/1 tsp sesame oil
5ml/1 tsp clear honey

SERVES 4

2 Tuck the slices of onion and the
apricots inside the pocket and press
the breast firmly back into shape.
Secure with metal skewers.

3 Mix together the clear honey and
sesame oil and brush generously over
the duck, particularly the skin. Sprinkle
over the star anise and season with
plenty of salt and fresh black pepper.

4 To make the salad, mix together
the shredded Chinese leaves, bean
sprouts and shredded spring onions
in a large bowl.

5 Shake together all the salad
dressing ingredients in a screw-topped
jar. Season to taste with salt and
pepper. Toss into the salad.

6 Cook the duck over a medium-hot
barbecue for 12–15 minutes, turning
once, until golden brown. The duck
should be slightly pink in the centre.

Cook's Tip

If you prefer not to eat the bean
sprouts raw, they can be blanched
by plunging them into boiling
water for 1 minute. Drain and
refresh in cold water.

1 Place the duck breasts, skin-side
down, on a chopping board or clean
work surface and cut a long slit down
one side with a sharp kitchen knife,
cutting not quite through, to form
a large pocket.

DUCK BREASTS WITH RED PEPPER JELLY GLAZE

. . .

Sweet potatoes have pinkish skins and flesh varying from creamy white to deep orange.
Choose a long cylindrical tuber to make neat round slices for this Cajun dish.

INGREDIENTS

2 duck breasts
1 sweet potato, about 400g/14oz
30ml/2 tbsp red pepper jelly
15ml/1 tbsp sherry vinegar
50g/2oz/4 tbsp butter, melted
coarse sea salt and freshly ground
black pepper

SERVES 2

4 Meanwhile, warm the red pepper jelly and sherry vinegar together in a bowl set over a saucepan of hot water, stirring to mix them as the jelly melts. Brush the skin of the duck with this jelly glaze and return to the barbecue, skin-side down, for a further 2–3 minutes to caramelize it.

5 Brush the sweet potato slices with melted butter and sprinkle with coarse sea salt. Cook on a hot barbecue for 8–10 minutes until soft, brushing with more butter and sprinkling with salt and pepper when you turn them. Serve the duck sliced with the sweet potatoes and accompany with a green salad.

1 Slash the skin of the duck breasts diagonally at 2.5cm/1in intervals and rub plenty of salt and pepper over the skin and into the cuts.

2 Scrub the sweet potato and cut into 1cm/½in slices, discarding the ends.

3 Cook the duck breasts on a medium barbecue, skin-side down, for 5 minutes. Turn and cook for a further 8–10 minutes, according to how pink you like your duck.

DUCK BREASTS WITH RED PLUMS
· · ·

The rich fruity sauce for this dish combines brandy and red plums with double cream and coriander. The sauce can be made in a pan on the barbecue while the duck is cooking.

INGREDIENTS
4 duck breasts, about 175g/6oz each, skinned
10ml/2 tsp crushed cinnamon stick
50g/2oz/¼ cup butter
15ml/1 tbsp plum brandy or Cognac
250ml/8fl oz/1 cup chicken stock
250ml/8fl oz/1 cup double cream
6 fresh red plums, stoned and sliced
6 sprigs fresh coriander leaves, plus extra to garnish
salt and freshly ground black pepper

SERVES 4

1 Score the duck breasts and sprinkle with salt. Press the crushed cinnamon on to both sides of the duck breasts. Brush with butter and cook on a medium barbecue for 15–20 minutes, turning once, until the duck is tender.

2 To make the sauce, melt half the remaining butter in a saucepan. Add the brandy or Cognac and set it alight. When the flames have died down, add the stock and cream and allow to simmer gently until reduced and thick. Add seasoning to taste.

3 In a saucepan, melt the other half of the butter and fry the plums and coriander just enough to cook the fruit through. Slice the duck breasts and pour some sauce around each one, then garnish with the plum slices and the chopped fresh coriander.

JUNIPER-SPICED VENISON CHOPS

∘ ∘ ∘

Depending on the type of venison available, the chops will vary in size, so you will need either one or two per person.

INGREDIENTS

4–8 venison chops
250ml/8 fl oz/1 cup red wine
2 medium red onions
6 juniper berries, crushed
1 cinnamon stick, crumbled
1 dried bay leaf, crumbled
thinly pared strip of orange rind
olive oil, for brushing
salt and freshly ground black pepper

SERVES 4

2 Add the juniper berries, cinnamon, bay leaf and orange rind. Toss well to coat evenly and then cover the bowl and leave to marinate for at least an hour, or overnight in the fridge.

1 Place the venison chops in a large mixing bowl and pour over the red wine. Using a sharp knife, cut the red onions in half crossways and add them to the bowl.

3 Drain the venison and onions and reserve the marinade. Brush the venison and onions generously with the olive oil and sprinkle with plenty of salt and freshly ground black pepper.

4 Cook the venison and onions on a medium-hot barbecue for about 8–10 minutes on each side, turning once and basting regularly with the marinade. The venison should still be slightly pink inside even when fully cooked.

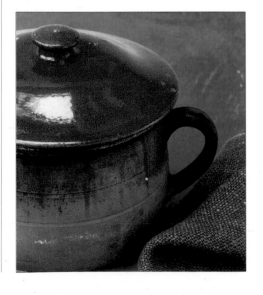

Cook's Tip

Tender farmed venison is now widely available from supermarkets and good butchers shops, but if venison is difficult to find, beef steaks could be used instead.

FISH AND SEAFOOD

Cooking over charcoal adds a marvellous flavour to fish and seafood, and it's very quick and easy to prepare this way. Oily fish such as mackerel, sardines or tuna are perfectly suited to grilling and won't dry out, while char-grilling will enhance their robust flavours. Use plump prawns or firm meaty-textured fish such as monkfish or swordfish for kebabs, but marinate them first to keep them moist. More delicate fish, or those that are best cooked in their own steam, can also be barbecued very successfully: just wrap them securely in foil and cook them either on the rack or directly on the coals. You can include all kinds of flavourings in the foil parcels, too.

MACKEREL KEBABS WITH SWEET PEPPER SALAD
◦ ◦ ◦

Mackerel is an excellent fish for barbecuing because its natural oils keep it moist and tasty.
This recipe combines mackerel with peppers and tomatoes in a flavoursome summer salad.

INGREDIENTS

4 medium mackerel, about
225g/8oz each, filleted
2 small red onions, cut in wedges
30ml/2 tbsp chopped fresh
marjoram
60ml/4 tbsp dry white wine
45ml/3 tbsp olive oil
juice of 1 lime

FOR THE SALAD
1 red pepper
1 yellow pepper
1 small red onion
2 large plum tomatoes
15ml/1 tbsp chopped fresh
marjoram
10ml/2 tsp balsamic vinegar
salt and freshly ground black
pepper

SERVES 4

1 Thread each mackerel fillet on to a skewer, with an onion wedge on each end. Arrange the skewers in a dish.

2 Mix together the marjoram, wine, oil and lime juice and spoon over the mackerel. Cover and chill in the fridge for at least 30 minutes, turning once.

3 To make the salad, quarter and seed both peppers and halve the onion. Place the peppers and onion, skin-side down, with the whole tomatoes, on a hot barbecue and leave until the skins are blackened and charred.

4 Remove the vegetables from the barbecue and leave until they are cool enough to handle. Use a sharp knife to peel off and discard the skins.

5 Chop the vegetables roughly and put them in a bowl. Stir in the marjoram and balsamic vinegar and season to taste. Toss thoroughly.

6 Remove the kebabs from the fridge and cook on a hot barbecue for about 10–12 minutes, turning occasionally and basting with the marinade. Serve with the pepper salad.

Cook's Tip
Other oily fish can be used for this dish: try fillets or cubes of herring, rainbow trout or salmon, instead.

SWORDFISH KEBABS
∘ ∘ ∘

Swordfish has a firm meaty texture that makes it ideal for cooking on a barbecue.
Marinade the fish first to keep it moist.

INGREDIENTS

900g/2lb swordfish steaks
45ml/3 tbsp olive oil
juice of ½ lemon
1 garlic clove, crushed
5ml/1 tsp paprika
3 tomatoes, quartered
2 onions, cut into wedges
salt and freshly ground black
pepper
salad and pitta bread, to serve

SERVES 4–6

1 Use a large kitchen knife to cut the swordfish steaks into large cubes. Arrange the cubes in a single layer in a large shallow dish.

2 Blend together the olive oil, lemon juice, garlic, paprika and seasoning in a bowl, and pour over the fish. Cover the dish loosely with clear film and leave to marinate in a cool place for up to 2 hours.

3 Thread the fish cubes on to metal skewers, alternating them with the pieces of tomato and onion wedges.

4 Cook the kebabs on a hot barbecue for about 5–10 minutes, basting frequently with the remaining marinade and turning occasionally. Serve with salad and pitta bread.

CALAMARI WITH TWO-TOMATO STUFFING

• • •

*Calamari, or baby squid, are quick to cook, but do turn and baste them often
and take care not to overcook them.*

INGREDIENTS

500g/1¼ lb baby squid, cleaned
1 garlic clove, crushed
*3 plum tomatoes, skinned and
chopped*
*8 sun-dried tomatoes in oil,
drained and chopped*
*60ml/4 tbsp chopped fresh basil,
plus extra, to serve*
*60ml/4 tbsp fresh white
breadcrumbs*
45ml/3 tbsp olive oil
15ml/1 tbsp red wine vinegar
*salt and freshly ground black
pepper*
lemon juice, to serve

SERVES 4

1 Remove the tentacles from the
squid and roughly chop them; leave
the main part of the squid whole.

2 Mix together the crushed garlic,
plum tomatoes, sun-dried tomatoes,
chopped fresh basil and breadcrumbs.
Stir in 15ml/1 tbsp of the olive oil and
the vinegar. Season well with plenty of
salt and freshly ground black pepper.
Soak some wooden cocktail sticks in
water for 10 minutes before use, to
prevent them burning on the barbecue.

3 Using a teaspoon, fill the squid
with the stuffing mixture. Secure the
open ends with the cocktail sticks to
hold the stuffing mixture in place.

4 Brush the squid with the remaining
olive oil and cook over a medium-hot
barbecue for 4–5 minutes, turning
often. Sprinkle with lemon juice and
extra chopped fresh basil to serve.

BARBECUED SCALLOPS WITH LIME BUTTER

. . .

*Fresh scallops are quick to cook and ideal for barbecues. This recipe combines them
simply with lime and fennel.*

INGREDIENTS

1 head fennel
2 limes
12 large scallops, cleaned
1 egg yolk
90ml/6 tbsp melted butter
olive oil for brushing
salt and freshly ground
black pepper

SERVES 4

3 Place the egg yolk and remaining lime rind and juice in a small bowl and whisk until pale and smooth.

5 Brush the fennel wedges with olive oil and cook them on a hot barbecue for 3–4 minutes, turning once.

1 Trim any feathery leaves from the fennel and reserve them. Slice the rest lengthways into thin wedges.

4 Gradually whisk in the melted butter and continue whisking until thick and smooth. Finely chop the reserved fennel leaves and stir them in, with seasoning to taste.

6 Add the scallops and cook for a further 3–4 minutes, turning once. Serve with the lime and fennel butter and the lime wedges.

2 Cut one lime into wedges. Finely grate the rind and squeeze the juice of the other lime and toss half the juice and rind on to the scallops. Season well with salt and fresh black pepper.

Cook's Tip

If the scallops are small, you may wish to thread them on to flat skewers to make turning them easier.

SARDINES WITH WARM HERB SALSA

Plain grilling is the very best way to cook fresh sardines. Served with this luscious herb salsa the only other essential item is fresh, crusty bread, to mop up the tasty juices.

INGREDIENTS

12–16 fresh sardines
oil for brushing
juice of 1 lemon

FOR THE SALSA
15ml/1 tbsp butter
4 spring onions, chopped
1 garlic clove, finely chopped
rind of 1 lemon
30ml/2 tbsp finely chopped fresh parsley
30ml/2 tbsp finely snipped fresh chives
30ml/2 tbsp finely chopped fresh basil
30ml/2 tbsp green olive paste
10ml/2 tsp balsamic vinegar
salt and freshly ground black pepper

SERVES 4

1 To clean the sardines, use a pair of small kitchen scissors to slit the fish along the belly and pull out the innards. Wipe the fish with kitchen paper and then arrange on a grill rack.

2 To make the salsa, melt the butter in a small pan and gently sauté the spring onions and garlic for about 2 minutes, shaking the pan occasionally, until softened but not browned.

3 Add the lemon rind and remaining salsa ingredients to the onions and garlic in the pan and keep warm on the edge of the barbecue, stirring occasionally. Do not allow to boil.

4 Brush the sardines lightly with oil and sprinkle with lemon juice, salt and pepper. Cook for about 2 minutes on each side, over a moderate heat. Serve with the warm salsa and crusty bread.

STUFFED SARDINES

° ° °

This Middle Eastern-inspired dish doesn't take much preparation and is a meal in itself.
Just serve with a crisp green salad tossed in a fresh lemon vinaigrette to make it complete.

INGREDIENTS

10g/¹⁄4 oz fresh parsley
3–4 garlic cloves, crushed
8–12 fresh or frozen sardines,
prepared
30ml/2 tbsp lemon juice
50g/2oz plain flour
2.5ml/¹⁄2 tsp ground cumin
olive oil, for brushing
salt and freshly ground black
pepper
naan bread and green salad,
to serve

SERVES 4

1 Finely chop the parsley and mix
in a small bowl with the garlic. Pat the
parsley and garlic mixture all over the
outsides and insides of the prepared
sardines. Sprinkle the sardines with
lemon juice, then place them in a dish,
cover and set aside in a cool place for
up to 2 hours, to absorb the flavours.

2 Place the flour on a large plate and
season with the cumin, salt and pepper.
Roll the sardines in the flour.

3 Brush the sardines with olive oil
and cook on a medium-hot barbecue
for about 3 minutes each side. Serve
with naan bread and a green salad.

MONKFISH WITH PEPPERED CITRUS MARINADE

∘ ∘ ∘

Monkfish is a firm, meaty fish that cooks well on the barbecue and keeps its shape.
Serve with a green salad.

INGREDIENTS

2 monkfish tails, about
350g/12oz each
1 lime
1 lemon
2 oranges
handful of fresh thyme sprigs
30ml/2 tbsp olive oil
15ml/1 tbsp mixed peppercorns,
roughly crushed
salt and freshly ground
black pepper

SERVES 4

2 Turn the fish and repeat on the other side, to remove the second fillet. Repeat on the second tail. (If you prefer, you can ask your fishmonger to do this for you.) Lay the four fillets out flat on a chopping board.

5 Squeeze the juice from the citrus fruits and mix it with the olive oil and more salt and pepper. Spoon over the fish. Cover with clear film and leave to marinate in the fridge for about 1 hour, turning occasionally and spooning the marinade over the fish.

1 Using a sharp kitchen knife, remove any skin from the monkfish tails. Cut carefully down one side of the backbone, sliding the knife between the bone and flesh, to remove the fillet on one side.

3 Cut two slices from each of the citrus fruits and arrange them over two of the fillets. Add a few sprigs of fresh thyme and sprinkle with plenty of salt and freshly ground black pepper. Finely grate the rind from the remaining fruit and sprinkle it over the fish.

6 Drain the monkfish, reserving the marinade, and sprinkle with the crushed peppercorns. Cook on a medium-hot barbecue for 15–20 minutes, basting with the marinade and turning occasionally, until the fish is evenly cooked.

4 Lay the other two fillets on top and tie them firmly at intervals.

CHAR-GRILLED TUNA WITH FIERY PEPPER PUREE

. . .

Tuna is an oily fish that barbecues well and is meaty enough to combine successfully with strong flavours – even hot chilli, as in this red pepper purée, which is excellent served with crusty bread.

INGREDIENTS

4 tuna steaks, about 175g/6oz each
finely grated rind and juice of 1 lime
30ml/2 tbsp olive oil
salt and freshly ground black pepper
lime wedges, to serve

FOR THE PEPPER PURÉE
2 red peppers, halved
45ml/3 tbsp olive oil, plus extra for
brushing
1 small onion
2 garlic cloves, crushed
2 red chillies
1 slice white bread without crusts,
diced
salt

SERVES 4

2 To make the pepper purée, brush the pepper halves with a little olive oil and cook them, skin-side down, on a hot barbecue, until the skin is charred and blackened. Place the onion in its skin on the barbecue and cook until browned, turning it occasionally.

3 Leave the peppers and onion until cool enough to handle, then remove the skins, using a sharp kitchen knife.

4 Place the cooked peppers and onion with the garlic, chillies, bread and olive oil in a food processor. Process until smooth. Add salt to taste.

5 Drain the tuna steaks from the marinade and cook them on a hot barbecue for 8–10 minutes, turning once, until golden brown. Serve the steaks with the pepper purée and lime wedges, with crusty bread if liked.

1 Trim any skin from the tuna and place the steaks in a single layer in a wide dish. Sprinkle over the lime rind and juice, olive oil, salt and black pepper. Cover with clear film and chill in the fridge until required.

Cook's Tip
The pepper purée can be made in advance, cooking the peppers and onion under a hot grill; keep it in the fridge until you cook the fish.

TROUT WITH BACON

∘ ∘ ∘

*The smoky, savoury flavour of crispy grilled bacon perfectly complements
the delicate flesh of the trout in this simple dish.*

INGREDIENTS

*4 trout, cleaned and gutted
25g/1oz/1 tbsp plain flour
4 rashers smoked streaky bacon
30ml/2 tbsp olive oil
juice of ½ lemon
salt and freshly ground
black pepper*

SERVES 4

1 Place the trout on a chopping
board and pat dry with kitchen paper.
Season the flour with the salt and
freshly ground black pepper. Stretch
the bacon rashers out thinly using the
back of a heavy kitchen knife.

2 Roll the fish in the seasoned flour
mixture and wrap tightly in the streaky
bacon. Brush with olive oil and cook
on a medium-hot barbecue for 10–15
minutes, turning once. Serve at once,
with the lemon juice drizzled on top.

120

RED MULLET WITH BASIL AND CITRUS

This Italian recipe is full of the warm, distinctive flavours of the Mediterranean.
Serve the dish with plain boiled rice and a green salad, or with lots of fresh crusty bread.

INGREDIENTS

4 red mullet, about 225g/8oz each,
filleted
60ml/4 tbsp olive oil
10 peppercorns, crushed
2 oranges, one peeled and sliced
and one squeezed
1 lemon
15g/½ oz/1 tbsp butter
2 drained canned anchovies,
chopped
60ml/4 tbsp shredded fresh basil
salt and freshly ground black
pepper

SERVES 4

1 Place the fish fillets in a shallow dish in a single layer. Pour over the olive oil and sprinkle with the crushed peppercorns. Lay the orange slices on top of the fish. Cover the dish with clear film, and leave to marinate in the fridge for at least 4 hours.

2 Halve the lemon. Remove the skin and pith from one half using a small, sharp knife, and slice the flesh thinly. Squeeze the juice from the other half.

3 Drain the fish, reserving the marinade and orange slices, and cook on a medium-hot barbecue for about 10–12 minutes, turning once and basting with the marinade.

4 Melt the butter in a saucepan with any remaining marinade. Add the chopped anchovies and cook until completely soft. Stir in the orange and lemon juice and allow to simmer on the edge of the barbecue until slightly reduced. Stir in the basil and check the seasoning. Pour over the fish and garnish with the reserved orange slices and the lemon slices.

FISH PARCELS

○ ○ ○

Sea bass is good for this recipe, but you could also use small whole trout or a white fish fillet such as cod or haddock.

INGREDIENTS

4 pieces sea bass fillet, or 4 small sea bass, about 450g/1lb each
olive oil for brushing
2 shallots, thinly sliced
1 garlic clove, chopped
15ml/1 tbsp capers
6 sun-dried tomatoes, finely chopped
4 black olives, stoned and thinly sliced
grated rind and juice of 1 lemon
5ml/1 tsp paprika
salt and freshly ground black pepper

SERVES 4

1 Clean the fish if whole. Cut four squares of double-thickness baking foil, large enough to enclose the fish; brush lightly with a little olive oil.

2 Place a piece of fish in the centre of each piece of baking foil and season well with plenty of salt and pepper.

3 Scatter over the shallots, chopped garlic, capers, tomatoes, sliced olives and grated lemon rind. Sprinkle with the lemon juice and paprika.

4 Fold over the baking foil to enclose the fish loosely, sealing the edges firmly so that none of the juices can escape during cooking. Place the parcels on a moderately hot barbecue and cook for about 8–10 minutes. To serve, place each of the parcels on a plate and loosen the tops to open.

Cook's Tip
These parcels can also be baked in the oven: place them on a baking sheet and cook at 200°C/400°F/Gas 6 for about 15–20 minutes.

HALIBUT WITH FRESH TOMATO AND BASIL SALSA

* * *

Take care when cooking this dish as halibut has a tendency to break easily, especially when the skin has been removed. Season well to bring out the flavour of the fish and the taste of the sauce.

INGREDIENTS

4 halibut fillets, about 175g/6oz each
45ml/3 tbsp olive oil

FOR THE SALSA
1 medium tomato, roughly chopped
¼ red onion, finely chopped
1 small jalapeño pepper
30ml/2 tbsp balsamic vinegar
10 large fresh basil leaves
15ml/1 tbsp olive oil
salt and freshly ground black pepper

SERVES 4

1 To make the salsa, mix together the chopped tomato, red onion, jalapeño pepper and balsamic vinegar in a bowl. Slice the fresh basil leaves finely, using a sharp kitchen knife.

2 Stir the basil and the olive oil into the tomato mixture. Season to taste. Cover the bowl with clear film and leave to marinate for at least 3 hours.

3 Rub the halibut fillets with oil and season. Cook on a medium barbecue for 8 minutes, basting with oil and turning once. Serve with the salsa.

COD FILLET WITH FRESH MIXED-HERB CRUST

*Use fresh herbs and wholemeal breadcrumbs to make a delicious crisp crust for the fish.
Season the fish well and serve with large lemon wedges.*

INGREDIENTS

25g/1oz/2 tbsp butter
15ml/1 tbsp fresh chervil
*15ml/1 tbsp fresh parsley, plus
extra sprigs to garnish*
15ml/1 tbsp fresh chives
175g/6oz/3 cups breadcrumbs
*4 thick pieces of cod fillet, about
225g/8oz each, skinned*
15ml/1 tbsp olive oil
lemon wedges, to garnish
*salt and freshly ground black
pepper*

SERVES 4

1 Melt the butter and chop all the herbs finely, using a sharp knife. Brush the cod fillets with melted butter and mix any remaining butter with the breadcrumbs, fresh herbs and plenty of salt and freshly ground black pepper.

2 Press a quarter of the mixture on to each fillet, spreading evenly, and lightly sprinkle with olive oil. Cook on a medium barbecue for about 10 minutes, turning once. Serve the fish garnished with lemon wedges and the sprigs of fresh parsley.

GRILLED SNAPPER WITH HOT MANGO SALSA

° ° °

A ripe mango provides the basis for a deliciously rich fruity salsa. The dressing needs no oil and features the tropical flavours of coriander, ginger and chilli.

INGREDIENTS

350g/12oz new potatoes
3 eggs
115g/4oz French beans, topped, tailed and halved
4 red snapper, about 350g/12oz each, cleaned, scaled and gutted
30ml/2 tbsp olive oil
175g/6oz mixed lettuce leaves, such as frisée or Webb's
2 cherry tomatoes
salt and freshly ground black pepper

FOR THE SALSA

45ml/3 tbsp chopped fresh coriander
1 medium-sized ripe mango, peeled, stoned and diced
½ red chilli, seeded and chopped
2.5cm/1in fresh root ginger, grated
juice of 2 limes
generous pinch of celery salt

SERVES 4

1 Bring the potatoes to the boil in a large saucepan of salted water and simmer for 15–20 minutes. Drain.

2 Bring a second large saucepan of salted water to the boil. Put in the eggs and boil for 4 minutes, then add the beans and cook for a further 6 minutes, so that the eggs have had a total of 10 minutes. Drain and refresh the beans. Remove the eggs from the saucepan. Cool, then shell and cut into quarters.

3 Using a sharp knife, slash each snapper three times on either side. Brush with olive oil and cook on a medium-hot barbecue for 12 minutes, basting occasionally and turning once.

4 To make the salsa, place the chopped fresh coriander in a food processor. Add the mango chunks, chilli, grated ginger, lime juice and celery salt and process until smooth.

5 Dress the lettuce leaves with olive oil and distribute them evenly between four large plates.

6 Arrange the snapper on the lettuce and season to taste. Halve the new potatoes and distribute them with the beans, tomatoes and quartered hard-boiled eggs over the salad. Serve immediately, with the salsa.

Variation

If fresh mangoes are unavailable, use canned ones, draining well. Sea bream are also good served with this hot mango salsa.

SMOKED HADDOCK WITH QUICK PARSLEY SAUCE

∘ ∘ ∘

*Make any herb sauce by this method, making sure it is thickened and seasoned well to
complement the smoky flavour of the fish.*

INGREDIENTS

*4 smoked haddock fillets, about
225g/8oz each
75g/3oz/6 tbsp butter, softened
25g/1oz/2 tbsp plain flour
300ml/½ pint/1¼ cups milk
60ml/4 tbsp chopped fresh parsley
salt and freshly ground black
pepper*

SERVES 4

1 Smear the fish fillets on both sides
with 50g/2oz/4 tbsp of the butter.

2 Beat the remaining butter and flour
together to make a paste.

3 Cook the fish on a medium-hot
barbecue for about 10 minutes, turning
once. Meanwhile, to make the sauce,
heat the milk in a saucepan to just
below boiling point. Add the flour
mixture in small spoonfuls, whisking
constantly over the heat. Continue
until the sauce is smooth and thick.

4 Add the seasoning and chopped
fresh parsley to the saucepan and stir
well. Pour the parsley sauce over the
haddock fillets to serve.

SALMON WITH RED ONION MARMALADE

• • •

*Salmon barbecues well but is most successful when it is at least 2.5cm/1in thick. The red onion
marmalade is rich and delicious. Puréed blackcurrants work as well as crème de cassis.*

INGREDIENTS

*4 salmon steaks, about 175g/6oz
each
30ml/2 tbsp olive oil
salt and freshly ground black
pepper*

FOR THE RED ONION MARMALADE
*5 medium red onions, peeled and
finely sliced
50g/2oz/4 tbsp butter
175ml/6floz/³/4 cup red wine vinegar
50ml/2fl oz/¹/4 cup crème de cassis
50ml/2fl oz/¹/4 cup grenadine
50ml/2fl oz/¹/4 cup red wine*

SERVES 4

1 Use your hands to rub the olive oil
into the salmon flesh and season well
with plenty of salt and freshly ground
black pepper.

2 Melt the butter in a large heavy-
based saucepan and add the sliced
onions. Sauté the onions for 5 minutes
until golden brown.

3 Stir in the vinegar, crème de cassis,
grenadine and wine and continue to
cook for about 10 minutes until the
liquid has almost entirely evaporated
and the onions are glazed. Season well.

4 Brush the fish with a little more
oil, and cook on a medium barbecue
for about 6–8 minutes, turning once.

MEXICO BARBECUED SALMON

The sauce for this dish is vibrant with hot, sweet and sour flavours that permeate the fish before and during cooking.

INGREDIENTS

1 small red onion
1 garlic clove
6 plum tomatoes
25g/1oz/2 tbsp butter
45ml/3 tbsp tomato ketchup
30ml/2 tbsp Dijon mustard
30ml/2 tbsp dark brown sugar
15ml/1 tbsp runny honey
5ml/1 tbsp cayenne pepper
15ml/1 tbsp ancho chilli powder
15ml/1 tbsp paprika
15ml/1 tbsp Worcestershire sauce
4 salmon fillets, about 175g/6oz
each

SERVES 4

3 Melt the butter in a large, heavy-based saucepan and gently cook the onion and garlic until translucent.

4 Add the tomatoes to the saucepan and allow to simmer for 15 minutes.

5 Add the remaining ingredients, excluding the salmon, and simmer for a further 20 minutes. Pour the mixture into a food processor and blend until smooth. Leave to cool.

1 Using a sharp knife, finely chop the red onion and finely dice the garlic.

6 Brush the salmon with the sauce, and chill for at least 2 hours. Cook on a hot barbecue for 6 minutes, basting with the sauce and turning once.

2 Next, dice the plum tomatoes finely and set them aside.

VEGETARIAN DISHES AND VEGETABLES

Vegetables cooked on the barbecue acquire a richness and depth of flavour that will add an extra dimension to your meal. There are lots of ideas here for vegetable accompaniments to meat and fish dishes, as well as for substantial main dishes that everyone, vegetarian or not, will love. All vegetables can be cooked in foil parcels, but many are ideally suited to grilling on the barbecue: jacket potatoes, peppers, aubergines and corn on the cob are irresistible cooked over charcoal, or you can spear a mixture of vegetables on to skewers to make colourful and delicious kebabs. Barbecued vegetables can also be cooled and made into fabulous salads. They certainly shouldn't be an afterthought on your barbecue menu.

RED BEAN AND MUSHROOM BURGERS

*Vegetarians, vegans and meat-eaters alike will enjoy these healthy, low-fat veggie burgers.
With salad, pitta bread and Greek-style yogurt, they make a substantial meal.*

INGREDIENTS

15ml/1 tbsp olive oil
1 small onion, finely chopped
1 garlic clove, crushed
5ml/1 tsp ground cumin
5ml/1 tsp ground coriander
2.5ml/½ tsp ground turmeric
*115g/4oz/1½ cups finely chopped
mushrooms*
400g/14oz can red kidney beans
*30ml/2 tbsp chopped fresh
coriander*
wholemeal flour (optional)
olive oil, for brushing
*salt and freshly ground black
pepper*
Greek-style yogurt, to serve

SERVES 4

2 Add the chopped mushrooms and
cook, stirring, until softened and dry.
Remove the pan from the heat and
empty the contents into a large bowl.

3 Drain the beans thoroughly, place
them in a bowl and mash with a fork.

4 Stir the kidney beans into the
frying pan, with the chopped fresh
coriander, and mix thoroughly. Season
the mixture well with plenty of salt
and freshly ground black pepper.

5 Using floured hands, form the
mixture into four flat burger shapes.
If the mixture is too sticky to handle,
mix in a little wholemeal flour.

6 Lightly brush the burgers with
olive oil and cook on a hot barbecue
for 8–10 minutes, turning once, until
golden brown. Serve with a spoonful
of yogurt and a green salad, if liked.

1 Heat the olive oil in a frying pan
and fry the chopped onion and garlic
over a moderate heat, stirring, until
softened. Add the spices and cook for
a further minute, stirring continuously.

Cook's Tip
These burgers are not quite as
firm as meat burgers, and will need
careful handling on the barbecue.

BARBECUED GOAT'S CHEESE PIZZA

*Pizzas cooked on the barbecue have a beautifully crisp and golden base. The combination
of goat's cheese and red onion in this recipe makes for a flavoursome main course dish.*

2 Brush the dough round with olive
oil and place, oiled side down, on a
medium barbecue. Cook for about
6–8 minutes until firm and golden
underneath. Brush the uncooked side
with olive oil and turn the pizza over.

3 Mix together the passata and
red pesto and quickly spread over
the cooked side of the pizza, to within
about 1cm/½in of the edge. Arrange
the onion, tomatoes and cheese on top
and sprinkle with salt and pepper.

4 Cook the pizza for 10 minutes
more, until golden brown and crisp.
Sprinkle with fresh basil and serve.

INGREDIENTS

150g/5oz packet pizza-base mix
olive oil, for brushing
150ml/¼ pint/⅔ cup passata
30ml/2 tbsp red pesto
1 small red onion, thinly sliced
8 cherry tomatoes, halved
115g/4oz firm goat's cheese, thinly
sliced
handful shredded fresh basil leaves
salt and freshly ground black
pepper

SERVES 4

1 Make up the pizza dough
according to the directions on the
packet. Roll out the dough on a lightly
floured surface to a round of about
25cm/10in diameter.

RED ONION GALETTES
∘ ∘ ∘

If non-vegetarians are to eat these pretty puff pastry tarts, you can scatter some chopped anchovies over them before barbecuing to add extra piquancy.

INGREDIENTS

60–75ml/4–5 tbsp olive oil
500g/1¼ lb red onions, sliced
1 garlic clove, crushed
30ml/2 tbsp chopped fresh mixed herbs, such as thyme, parsley and basil
225g/8oz ready-made puff pastry
15ml/1 tbsp sun-dried tomato paste
freshly ground black pepper
fresh thyme sprigs, to garnish

SERVES 4

1 Heat 30ml/2 tbsp oil in a frying pan and add the onions and garlic. Cover and cook gently for 15–20 minutes, stirring occasionally, until soft but not browned. Stir in the herbs.

2 Divide the pastry into four and roll out each piece to a 15cm/6in round. Flute the edges, prick all over with a fork and place on baking sheets.

3 Chill the rounds, on the baking sheets, in the fridge for 10 minutes. Mix 15ml/1 tbsp of the remaining olive oil with the sun-dried tomato paste and spread over the pastry rounds, to within about 1cm/½ in of the edge.

4 Spread the onion mixture over the pastry and season with pepper. Drizzle over a little oil, then place the baking sheets on a medium barbecue for 15 minutes, until the pastry is crisp. Serve hot, garnished with thyme sprigs.

TOFU SATAY

· · ·

Grill cubes of tofu until crispy then serve with a Thai-style peanut sauce. Soak the satay sticks before use to prevent them burning while on the barbecue.

INGREDIENTS

2 × 200g/7oz packs smoked tofu
45ml/3 tbsp light soy sauce
10ml/2 tsp sesame oil
1 garlic clove, crushed
1 yellow and 1 red pepper, cut in
squares
8–12 fresh bay leaves
sunflower oil, for brushing

FOR THE PEANUT SAUCE
2 spring onions, finely chopped
2 garlic cloves, crushed
good pinch chilli powder, or a few
drops hot chilli sauce
5ml/1 tsp sugar
15ml/1 tbsp white wine vinegar
30ml/2 tbsp light soy sauce
45ml/3 tbsp crunchy peanut butter

SERVES 4–6

1 Cut the tofu into bite-sized cubes and place in a large bowl. Add the soy sauce, sesame oil and crushed garlic and mix well. Cover with clear film and marinate for at least 20 minutes.

2 Beat all the peanut sauce ingredients together in a large bowl, using a wooden spoon, until well blended. Avoid using a food processor to blend the ingredients, as the texture should be slightly chunky.

3 Drain the tofu and thread the cubes on to 8–12 satay sticks, alternating the tofu with the pepper squares and bay leaves. Larger bay leaves may need to be halved before threading.

4 Brush the satays with sunflower oil and cook on a hot barbecue or grill, turning the sticks occasionally, until the tofu and peppers are browned and crisp. Serve hot with the peanut sauce.

SWEET AND SOUR VEGETABLES WITH PANEER

° · ° °

The Indian cheese used in this recipe, called paneer, can be bought from Asian stores, or you can use tofu in its place. Paneer has a good firm texture and cooks very well on the barbecue.

INGREDIENTS

1 green pepper, cut into squares
1 yellow pepper, cut into squares
8 cherry, or 4 medium, tomatoes
8 cauliflower florets
8 fresh or canned pineapple chunks
8 cubes paneer

FOR THE SEASONED OIL
15ml/1 tbsp soya oil
30ml/2 tbsp lemon juice
5ml/1 tsp salt
5ml/1 tsp freshly ground black
pepper
15ml/1 tbsp clear honey
30ml/2 tbsp chilli sauce

SERVES 4

1 Thread the prepared vegetables, pineapple and paneer cubes on to four skewers, alternating the ingredients.

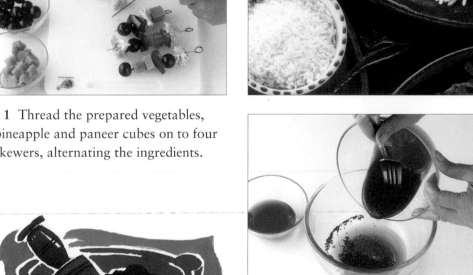

2 Mix together all the ingredients for the seasoned oil. If the mixture is a little too thick, add 15ml/1 tbsp water to loosen it. Brush the vegetables with the seasoned oil, ready for cooking.

3 Cook on a hot barbecue or grill for 10 minutes, until the vegetables begin to char slightly, turning the skewers often and basting with the seasoned oil. Serve on a bed of plain boiled rice.

VEGETABLE KEBABS WITH PEPPERCORN SAUCE

° ° °

Vegetables invariably taste good when cooked on the barbecue. You can include other vegetables in these kebabs, depending on what is available at the time.

INGREDIENTS

24 mushrooms
16 cherry tomatoes
16 large fresh basil leaves
2 courgettes, cut into 16 thick
slices
16 large fresh mint leaves
1 large red pepper, cut into
16 squares

TO BASTE
120ml/4fl oz/½ cup melted butter
1 garlic clove, crushed
15ml/1 tbsp crushed green
peppercorns
salt

FOR THE GREEN PEPPERCORN SAUCE
50g/2oz/¼ cup butter
45ml/3 tbsp brandy
250ml/8fl oz/1 cup double cream
5ml/1 tsp crushed green
peppercorns

SERVES 4

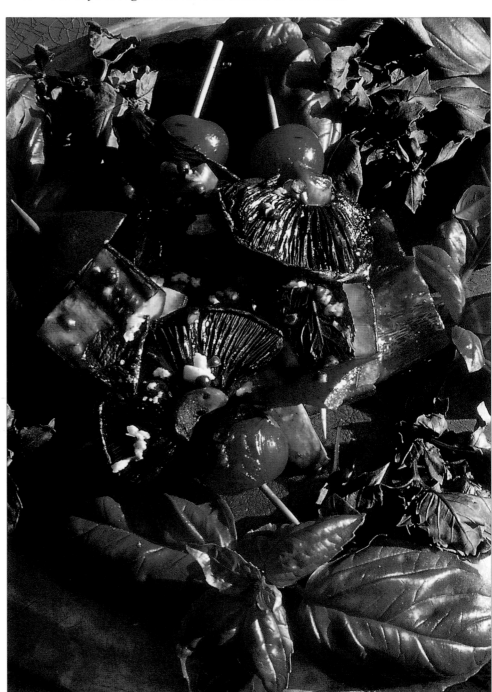

1 Thread the vegetables on to 8 bamboo skewers that you have soaked in water to prevent them burning. Place the fresh basil leaves immediately next to the tomatoes, and wrap the mint leaves around the courgette slices.

2 Mix the basting ingredients in a bowl and baste the kebabs thoroughly. Cook the skewers on a medium-hot barbecue, turning and basting regularly until the vegetables are just cooked – this should take about 5–7 minutes.

3 Heat the butter for the green peppercorn sauce in a frying pan, then add the brandy and light it. When the flames have died down, stir in the cream and the peppercorns. Cook for 2 minutes, stirring all the time. Serve the sauce with the barbecued kebabs.

CASSAVA AND VEGETABLE KEBABS
. . .

This is an attractive and delicious assortment of African vegetables, marinated in a spicy garlic sauce, then roasted over hot coals. If cassava is unavailable, use sweet potato or yam instead.

INGREDIENTS
175g/6oz cassava
1 onion, cut into wedges
1 aubergine, cut into bite-sized pieces
1 courgette, sliced
1 ripe plantain, sliced
½ red pepper and ½ green pepper, sliced
16 cherry tomatoes
rice or couscous, to serve

FOR THE MARINADE
60ml/4 tbsp lemon juice
60ml/4 tbsp olive oil
45–60ml/3–4 tbsp soy sauce
15ml/1 tbsp tomato paste
1 green chilli, seeded and finely chopped
½ onion, grated
2 garlic cloves, crushed
5ml/1 tsp mixed spice
pinch of dried thyme

SERVES 4

1 Peel the cassava and cut into bite-size pieces. Place in a large bowl, cover with boiling water and leave to blanch for about 5 minutes. Drain well.

2 Place all the prepared vegetables, including the cassava, in a large bowl and mix with your hands so that all the vegetables are evenly distributed.

3 Blend the marinade ingredients in a jug and pour over the vegetables. Cover and leave to marinate for 1–2 hours.

4 Thread the vegetables, with the cherry tomatoes, on to eight skewers and cook on a hot barbecue for about 15 minutes until tender and browned. Turn the skewers frequently and baste them occasionally with the marinade.

5 Meanwhile, pour the remaining marinade into a small saucepan and simmer for about 10 minutes to reduce. Strain the reduced marinade into a jug. Serve the kebabs on a bed of rice or couscous, with the sauce on the side.

BAKED SQUASH WITH PARMESAN

Almost all types of squash are suitable for barbecue cooking, and they are extemely easy to deal
with: simply wrap them in baking foil and place them in the hot embers until they soften.

INGREDIENTS
2 acorn or butternut squashes,
about 450g/1lb each
15ml/1 tbsp olive oil
50g/2oz/4 tbsp butter, melted
75g/3oz/1 cup grated Parmesan
cheese
60ml/4 tbsp pine nuts, toasted
salt and freshly ground black
pepper
2.5ml/½ tsp freshly grated nutmeg

SERVES 4

2 Brush the cut surfaces with oil and
sprinkle with salt and black pepper.

5 Dice the flesh, then stir in the
melted butter. Add the Parmesan, pine
nuts, salt and pepper. Toss well to mix.

1 Cut the squashes in half and scoop
out the seeds with a spoon.

3 Wrap each squash in baking foil
and place in the embers of the fire.
Cook for 25–30 minutes, until tender.
Turn the parcels occasionally so that
the squash cook evenly.

6 Spoon the mixture back into the
shells. Sprinkle with nutmeg to serve.

4 Leave the squash until cool enough
to handle. Unwrap the squashes from
the foil parcels and scoop out the flesh,
leaving the skins intact.

Cook's Tip
Spaghetti squash can also be
cooked in this way. Just scoop out
the spaghetti-like strands and toss
with butter and Parmesan cheese.

BAKED STUFFED COURGETTES

∘ ∘ ∘

The tangy goat's cheese stuffing contrasts well with the very delicate flavour of the courgettes in this recipe. Wrap the courgettes and bake them in the embers of the fire.

2 Insert pieces of goat's cheese in the slits. Add a little chopped mint and sprinkle over the oil and black pepper.

3 Wrap each courgette in foil, place in the embers of the fire and bake for about 25 minutes, until tender.

INGREDIENTS

8 small courgettes, about 450g/1lb total weight
15ml/1 tbsp olive oil, plus extra for brushing
75–115g/3–4oz goat's cheese, cut into thin strips
a few sprigs of fresh mint, finely chopped, plus extra to garnish
freshly ground black pepper

SERVES 4

1 Cut eight pieces of baking foil large enough to encase each courgette, and lightly brush each piece with olive oil. Trim the courgettes and cut a thin slit along the length of each.

Cook's Tip

While almost any cheese can be used in this recipe, mild cheeses such as Cheddar or mozzarella, will best allow the flavour of the courgettes to be appreciated.

VEGETABLE PARCELS WITH FLOWERY BUTTER

· · ·

Nasturtium leaves and flowers are edible and have a distinctive peppery flavour.
They make a pretty addition to summer barbecue dishes.

INGREDIENTS

200g/7oz baby carrots
250g/9oz yellow patty-pan
squashes or yellow courgettes
115g/4oz baby sweetcorn
1 onion, thinly sliced
50g/2oz/4 tbsp butter, plus extra
for greasing
finely grated rind of ½ lemon
6 young nasturtium leaves
4–8 nasturtium flowers
salt and freshly ground
black pepper

SERVES 4

1 Trim the vegetables with a sharp knife, leaving them whole unless they are very large – if necessary, cut them into even-size pieces.

2 Divide the vegetables between four double-thickness squares of buttered baking foil and season well.

3 Mix the butter with the lemon rind in a small bowl. Roughly chop the nasturtium leaves and add them to the butter. Place a generous spoonful of the butter on each pile of vegetables in the squares of baking foil.

4 Fold over the foil and seal the edges to make a neat parcel. Cook on a medium-hot barbecue for 30 minutes until the vegetables are tender. Open the parcels and top each with one or two nasturtium flowers. Serve at once.

STUFFED TOMATOES AND PEPPERS
. . .

Colourful peppers and tomatoes make perfect containers for meat and vegetable stuffings. The barbecued flavours in this dish are simply superb.

INGREDIENTS

2 large ripe tomatoes
1 green pepper
1 yellow or orange pepper
60ml/4 tbsp olive oil, plus extra for sprinkling
2 onions, chopped
2 garlic cloves, crushed
50g/2oz/1/2 cup blanched almonds, chopped
75g/3oz/scant 1/2 cup long grain rice, boiled and drained
30ml/2 tbsp fresh mint, roughly chopped
30ml/2 tbsp fresh parsley, roughly chopped
25g/1oz/2 tbsp sultanas
45ml/3 tbsp ground almonds
salt and freshly ground black pepper
chopped mixed fresh herbs, to garnish

SERVES 4

2   Halve the peppers, leaving the cores intact. Scoop out the seeds. Brush the peppers with 15ml/1 tbsp olive oil and cook on a medium barbecue for 15 minutes. Place the peppers and tomatoes on a grill rack and season well with salt and pepper.

3   Fry the onions in the remaining olive oil for 5 minutes. Add the crushed garlic and chopped almonds to the pan and fry for a further minute.

4   Remove the pan from the heat and stir in the rice, chopped tomatoes, mint, parsley and sultanas. Season well with salt and pepper and spoon the mixture into the tomatoes and peppers.

1   Cut the tomatoes in half and scoop out the pulp and seeds, using a teaspoon. Leave the tomatoes to drain on kitchen paper with the cut sides facing down. Roughly chop the tomato pulp and set it aside.

5   Scatter with the ground almonds and sprinkle with a little extra olive oil. Cook on a medium barbecue for about 15 minutes. Garnish with fresh herbs.

COUSCOUS STUFFED PEPPERS

· · ·

Couscous makes a good basis for a stuffing, and in this recipe it is studded with raisins and flavoured with fresh mint. Charred peppers make the combination of flavours truly special.

2 To cook the couscous, bring 250ml/8fl oz/1 cup water to the boil. Add the oil and salt, then remove from the heat and add the couscous. Stir and leave to stand, covered, for 5 minutes. Stir in the onion, raisins and mint. Season well and stir in the egg yolk.

3 Use a teaspoon to fill the peppers with the couscous mixture to about three-quarters full (the couscous will swell while cooking). Wrap each pepper in a piece of oiled baking foil.

4 Cook on a medium barbecue for 20 minutes, until tender. Serve hot or cold, garnished with fresh mint leaves.

INGREDIENTS

6 peppers
25g/1oz/2 tbsp butter
1 onion, finely chopped
5ml/1 tsp olive oil
2.5ml/½ tsp salt
175g/6oz/1 cup couscous
25g/1oz/2 tbsp raisins
30ml/2 tbsp chopped fresh mint
1 egg yolk
salt and freshly ground black pepper
mint leaves, to garnish

SERVES 4

1 Carefully slit each pepper with a sharp knife and remove the core and seeds. Melt the butter in a small saucepan and add the chopped onion. Cook until soft but not browned.

SWEETCORN IN A GARLIC BUTTER CRUST

° ° °

*Whether you are catering for vegetarians or serving this with meat dishes, it will disappear
in a flash. The charred garlic butter crust adds a new dimension to the corn cobs.*

INGREDIENTS

6 ripe corn cobs
225g/8oz/1 cup butter
30ml/2 tbsp olive oil
2 garlic cloves, crushed
115g/4oz/1 cup wholemeal
breadcrumbs
15ml/1 tbsp chopped fresh parsley
salt and freshly ground black
pepper

SERVES 6

1 Pull off the husks and silks and
boil the corn cobs in a large saucepan
of salted water until tender. Drain the
corn cobs and leave to cool.

2 Melt the butter in a saucepan and
add the olive oil, crushed garlic, salt
and freshly ground black pepper, and
stir to blend. Pour the mixture into a
shallow dish. In another shallow dish
blend the breadcrumbs and chopped
fresh parsley. Roll the corn cobs in the
melted butter mixture and then in the
breadcrumbs until they are well coated.

3 Cook the corn cobs on a hot
barbecue for about 10 minutes, turning
frequently, until the breadcrumbs are
golden brown.

STUFFED PARSLEYED ONIONS

These stuffed onions are a popular vegetarian dish served with fresh crusty bread and a crisp salad. They also make a very good accompaniment to meat dishes.

INGREDIENTS
4 large onions
60ml/4 tbsp cooked rice
20ml/4 tsp finely chopped fresh parsley, plus extra to garnish
60ml/4 tbsp strong Cheddar cheese, finely grated
30ml/2 tbsp olive oil
15ml/1 tbsp white wine
salt and freshly ground black pepper

SERVES 4

1 Cut a slice from the top of each onion and scoop out the centre to leave a fairly thick shell. Combine all the remaining ingredients in a large bowl and stir to mix, moistening with enough white wine to bind the ingredients together well.

2 Use a spoon to fill the onions, then wrap each one in a piece of oiled baking foil. Bake in the embers of the fire for 30–40 minutes, until tender, turning the parcels often so they cook evenly. Serve the onions garnished with chopped fresh parsley.

STUFFED ARTICHOKE BOTTOMS

*The distinctive flavour of char-grilled globe artichokes is matched in this dish by
an intensely savoury stuffing of mushrooms, cheese and walnuts.*

INGREDIENTS

225g/8oz button mushrooms
15g/½ oz/1 tbsp butter
2 shallots, finely chopped
*50g/2oz full- or medium-fat soft
cheese*
30ml/2 tbsp chopped walnuts
45ml/3 tbsp grated Gruyère cheese
*4 large or 6 small artichoke
bottoms (from cooked artichokes,
leaves and choke removed, or
cooked frozen or canned artichoke
hearts)*
*salt and freshly ground black
pepper*
fresh parsley sprigs, to garnish

SERVES 4

1 To make the duxelles for the
stuffing, put the mushrooms in a
food processor or blender and pulse
until finely chopped.

2 Melt the butter in a frying pan
and cook the shallots over a medium
heat for about 2–3 minutes until just
softened. Add the mushrooms, raise the
heat slightly, and cook for 5–7 minutes
more, stirring frequently, until all the
liquid from the mushrooms has been
driven off and they are almost dry.
Season with plenty of salt and freshly
ground black pepper.

3 In a large bowl, combine the soft
cheese and cooked mushrooms. Add
the chopped walnuts and half the
grated Gruyère cheese, and stir well
to combine the mixture.

4 Divide the mixture among the
artichoke bottoms arranged in an oiled
baking tin. Sprinkle over the remaining
cheese. Cook on the barbecue for 12
minutes, garnish with parsley and serve.

SPINACH WITH RAISINS AND PINE NUTS

Raisins and pine nuts are frequent partners in Spanish recipes. In this recipe they are tossed with wilted spinach and croûtons, and can be cooked quickly in a flameproof pan on the barbecue.

INGREDIENTS

50g/2oz/⅓ cup raisins
1 thick slice crusty white bread
45ml/3 tbsp olive oil
25g/1oz/⅓ cup pine nuts
500g/1¼ lb young spinach, stalks removed
2 garlic cloves, crushed
salt and freshly ground black pepper

SERVES 4

1 Put the raisins in a bowl, cover with boiling water and leave to soak for 10 minutes. Drain and set aside.

2 Cut the bread into cubes and discard the crusts. Heat 30ml/2 tbsp of the olive oil in a large frying pan and fry the bread until golden brown.

3 Heat the remaining oil and fry the pine nuts, on the barbecue or hob, until beginning to colour. Add the spinach and garlic and cook quickly, turning the spinach until it has just wilted. Toss in the raisins and season lightly with salt and pepper. Transfer to a serving dish. Scatter with croûtons and serve.

GRILLED VEGETABLE TERRINE

A colourful, layered terrine, using all the vegetables associated with the Mediterranean, makes a successful and elegant dish for outdoor eating. Barbecuing the vegetables adds to the flavour.

INGREDIENTS

2 large red peppers, quartered,
cored and seeded
2 large yellow peppers, quartered,
cored and seeded
1 large aubergine, sliced lengthways
2 large courgettes, sliced
lengthways
90ml/6 tbsp olive oil
1 large red onion, thinly sliced
75g/3oz/½ cup raisins
15ml/1 tbsp tomato purée
15ml/1 tbsp red wine vinegar
400ml/14fl oz/1²/₃ cups tomato
juice
15g/½oz/2 tbsp powdered gelatine
fresh basil leaves, to garnish

FOR THE DRESSING
90ml/6 tbsp extra virgin olive oil
30ml/2 tbsp red wine vinegar
salt and freshly ground black
pepper

SERVES 6

1 Grill the peppers, skin-side down, on a hot barbecue or grill, until the skins are beginning to blacken. Transfer to a bowl, cover and leave to cool.

2 Brush the aubergine and courgette slices with oil and cook until tender and golden, turning occasionally.

3 Heat the remaining oil in a pan and add the onion, raisins, tomato purée and red wine vinegar. Cook until soft and syrupy. Leave to cool in the pan.

4 Pour half the tomato juice into a saucepan and sprinkle with the gelatine. Dissolve gently over a very low heat, stirring continuously.

5 Line an oiled 1.75 litre/3 pint/ 7½ cup terrine with clear film, leaving a little hanging over the sides. Place a layer of red peppers in the bottom and pour in enough of the tomato juice with gelatine to cover. Repeat with the aubergines, courgettes, yellow peppers and onion mixture, ending with another layer of red peppers and covering each layer with tomato juice and gelatine.

6 Add the remaining tomato juice to any left in the pan and pour into the terrine. Give it a sharp tap to eliminate air bubbles. Cover the terrine with clear film and chill until set.

7 To make the dressing, whisk the oil and vinegar, and season with salt and black pepper. Turn out the terrine and serve in thick slices, drizzled with the dressing. Garnish with the basil leaves.

WILD RICE WITH VEGETABLES

∘ ∘ ∘

*Wild rice makes a special accompaniment to barbecued vegetables in a simple vinaigrette
dressing. This recipe can be served as a side dish, but it also makes a tasty meal on its own.*

INGREDIENTS

*225g/8oz/1 cup wild and long
grain rice mixture
1 large aubergine, thickly sliced
1 red, 1 yellow and 1 green pepper,
quartered, cored and seeded
2 red onions, sliced
225g/8oz shiitake mushrooms
2 small courgettes, cut in half
lengthways
olive oil, for brushing
30ml/2 tbsp chopped fresh thyme*

FOR THE DRESSING
*90ml/6 tbsp extra virgin olive oil
30ml/2 tbsp balsamic vinegar
2 garlic cloves, crushed
salt and freshly ground black
pepper*

SERVES 4

1 Put the wild and long grain rice
mixture in a pan of cold salted water.
Bring to the boil, then reduce the heat,
cover and cook gently for about 30–40
minutes until the grains are tender (or
follow the cooking instructions on the
packet, if appropriate).

2 To make the dressing, mix together
the olive oil, vinegar, crushed garlic and
seasoning in a bowl or screw-topped
jar until well blended.

3 Arrange the vegetables on a rack.
Brush with olive oil and cook on a hot
barbecue or grill for 8–10 minutes,
until tender and well browned, turning
them occasionally and basting with oil.

4 Drain the rice and toss in half the
dressing. Tip into a serving dish and
arrange the grilled vegetables on top.
Pour over the remaining dressing and
scatter over the chopped fresh thyme.

POTATO SKEWERS WITH MUSTARD DIP

· · ·

Potatoes cooked on the barbecue have a tasty flavour and crisp skin.
These skewers are served with a thick, garlic-rich dip.

INGREDIENTS

1kg/2¼lb small new potatoes
200g/7oz/2 cups shallots, halved
30ml/2 tbsp olive oil
15ml/1 tbsp sea salt

FOR THE MUSTARD DIP
4 garlic cloves, crushed
2 egg yolks
30ml/2 tbsp lemon juice
300ml/½ pint/1¼ cups extra
virgin olive oil
10ml/2 tsp whole-grain mustard
salt and freshly ground black
pepper

SERVES 4

1 To make the mustard dip, place the garlic, egg yolks and lemon juice in a blender or food processor and process for a few seconds until smooth.

2 With the motor running, add the oil, until the mixture forms a thick cream. Add the mustard and season.

3 Par-boil the potatoes in salted boiling water for about 5 minutes. Drain well and then thread them on to metal skewers with the shallots.

4 Brush with olive oil and sprinkle with sea salt. Cook for 10–12 minutes over a hot barbecue, turning often, until tender. Serve with the mustard dip.

SALADS AND ACCOMPANIMENTS

———✦———

Cool salads are a perfect foil to barbecued food, but they

should have assertive characters of their own. The recipes that

follow include some marvellous sunny, Mediterranean flavours that

taste especially good on summer days, and a selection of them would

be perfect as part of a buffet for a party. Don't forget that you can use

the barbecue to grill ingredients such as tomatoes, peppers, aubergines

and radicchio – it will give them an intense, smoky flavour that

will pervade the whole salad.

APPLE COLESLAW

There are many variations of this traditional salad; this recipe combines the sweet flavours of apple and carrot with a hint of celery. Prepare the salad in advance and chill until needed.

INGREDIENTS
450g/1lb white cabbage
1 medium onion
2 apples, peeled and cored
175g/6oz carrots, peeled
150ml/5fl oz/²⁄₃ cup mayonnaise
5ml/1 tsp celery salt
freshly ground black pepper

SERVES 4

1 Remove the outer leaves from the white cabbage and, using a heavy knife, cut it into 5cm/2in wedges. Remove and discard the stem sections.

2 Feed the cabbage wedges and the onion through the slicing blade of a food processor. Change to a grating blade and grate the apples and carrots. If you do not have a food processor, use a vegetable slicer and a hand grater.

3 Combine the salad ingredients in a large mixing bowl. Fold in the mayonnaise and season with celery salt and freshly ground black pepper.

Cook's Tip
This recipe can be adapted easily to suit different tastes. Add 125g/4oz/¹⁄₂ cup chopped walnuts or raisins for added texture, or, for a richer, more substantial coleslaw, add 125g/4oz/¹⁄₂ cup grated Cheddar cheese.

TOMATO AND FETA CHEESE SALAD

· · ·

Sweet sun-ripened tomatoes are rarely more delicious than when mixed with feta cheese and olive oil. This salad can be served with any barbecued meats, fish or vegetables.

INGREDIENTS

900g/2lb tomatoes
200g/7oz feta cheese
120ml/4fl oz/½ cup olive oil
12 black olives
4 sprigs fresh basil
freshly ground black pepper

SERVES 4

3 Crumble the feta cheese over the tomatoes, sprinkle with olive oil, then sprinkle with olives and fresh basil. Season with freshly ground black pepper and serve at room temperature.

1 Remove the tough cores from the tomatoes with a small kitchen knife.

2 Slice the tomatoes thickly on a chopping board and arrange the slices in a wide-based shallow dish.

Cook's Tip
Feta cheese has a strong flavour and can be very salty. For an authentic flavour and texture, look out for Greek, Cypriot or Turkish feta.

CURLY ENDIVE SALAD WITH BACON

° ° °

When they are in season, young dandelion leaves could be included in this French salad.
If you wish, sprinkle the salad with chopped hard-boiled egg.

2 Heat 15ml/1 tbsp oil in a pan over a medium heat and add the bacon. Fry until browned. Remove the bacon and drain on kitchen paper.

3 Add another 30ml/2 tbsp oil to the pan and fry the bread cubes over a medium heat, turning frequently, until browned. Remove the bread cubes with a slotted spoon and drain on kitchen paper. Discard any remaining fat.

INGREDIENTS

225g/8oz/6 cups curly endive or
escarole leaves
75–90ml/5–6 tbsp extra virgin
olive oil
175g/6oz piece of smoked bacon,
diced
thick slice white bread, cubed
1 small garlic clove, finely chopped
15ml/1 tbsp red wine vinegar
10ml/2 tsp Dijon mustard
salt and freshly ground black
pepper

SERVES 4

1 Tear the lettuce leaves into bite-size pieces and put them in a large salad bowl. Set the bowl aside.

4 Stir the garlic, vinegar and mustard into the pan with the remaining oil and warm through. Season to taste. Pour the dressing over the salad and sprinkle with the fried bacon and croûtons.

POTATO SALAD WITH SAUSAGE

· · ·

The addition of garlic sausage makes this a substantial salad to serve as part of a buffet, but if it is to accompany barbecued meat or fish you can make it with potatoes alone.

INGREDIENTS

450g/1lb small waxy potatoes
30–45ml/2–3 tbsp dry white wine
2 shallots, finely chopped
15ml/1 tbsp chopped fresh parsley
15ml/1 tbsp chopped fresh tarragon
175g/6oz French garlic sausage
fresh parsley, to garnish
salt and freshly ground black pepper

FOR THE VINAIGRETTE
10ml/2 tsp Dijon mustard
15ml/1 tbsp tarragon vinegar or white wine vinegar
75ml/5 tbsp extra virgin olive oil

SERVES 4

1 Cook the potatoes in boiling salted water for 10–15 minutes, until tender. Drain them, and refresh under cold running water. Cut them into 5mm/ ¼ in slices, place them in a large bowl and sprinkle with the white wine and the chopped shallots.

2 To make the vinaigrette, mix the Dijon mustard and vinegar in a small bowl, then whisk in the olive oil, 15ml/1 tbsp at a time. Season well with salt and freshly ground black and pour over the potatoes.

3 Add the chopped fresh parsley and tarragon to the potatoes in the bowl and toss until well mixed.

4 Slice the garlic sausage thinly and toss with the potatoes. Season with salt and pepper to taste and serve at room temperature, garnished with parsley.

GREEN BEAN SALAD WITH EGG TOPPING

∘ ∘ ∘

*When green beans are fresh and plentiful, serve them lightly cooked as a salad topped with
butter-fried breadcrumbs, egg and fresh parsley.*

INGREDIENTS

*675g/1½ lb green beans, topped
and tailed*
30ml/2 tbsp extra virgin olive oil
30ml/2 tbsp butter
*50g/2oz/1 cup fresh white
breadcrumbs*
60ml/4 tbsp chopped fresh parsley
1 egg, hard-boiled and shelled
salt

SERVES 4

1 Bring a large pan of salted water to
the boil. Add the beans and cook for 6
minutes. Drain well, toss the beans in
olive oil and allow to cool.

2 Heat the butter in a large frying
pan, add the breadcrumbs and fry until
golden. Remove the frying pan from
the heat, add the chopped fresh parsley,
then grate in the hard-boiled egg.

3 Place the beans in a shallow
serving dish and spoon on the
breadcrumb topping. If preparing the
salad in advance and chilling it in the
fridge until needed, allow it to come
to room temperature before serving.

TABBOULEH

◦ ◦ ◦

This classic Lebanese salad has become very popular everywhere. It makes an ideal substitute
for a rice dish and is especially good with barbecued lamb.

INGREDIENTS

175g/6oz/1 cup fine bulgur wheat
juice of 1 lemon
45ml/3 tbsp olive oil
40g/1½ oz fresh parsley, finely
chopped
45ml/3 tbsp fresh mint, chopped
4–5 spring onions, chopped
1 green pepper, sliced
salt and freshly ground black
pepper
2 large tomatoes, diced, and black
olives, to garnish

SERVES 4

1 Put the bulgur wheat in a large bowl. Add enough cold water to cover the wheat and let it stand for at least 30 minutes and up to 2 hours.

2 Drain and squeeze the wheat with your hands to remove excess water. The bulgur wheat will swell to double its original size. Spread the wheat on kitchen paper to allow to dry completely.

3 Place the bulgur wheat in a large bowl, add the lemon juice, the olive oil and a little salt and pepper. Allow to stand for 1–2 hours if possible, in order for the flavours to develop.

4 Add the chopped parsley, mint, spring onions and pepper to the wheat in the bowl and mix well. Garnish with diced tomatoes and olives and serve. The tabbouleh can be prepared in advance, covered with clear film and stored in the fridge until needed.

177

PEPPERS WITH TOMATOES AND ANCHOVIES

• • •

This is a Sicilian-style salad full of warm Mediterranean flavours. The salad improves if it is made and dressed an hour or two before serving.

INGREDIENTS

1 red pepper
1 yellow pepper
4 ripe plum tomatoes, sliced
2 canned anchovies, drained and chopped
4 sun-dried tomatoes in oil, drained and sliced
15ml/1 tbsp capers, drained
15ml/1 tbsp pine nuts
1 garlic clove, very finely sliced

FOR THE DRESSING
75ml/5 tbsp extra virgin olive oil
15ml/1 tbsp balsamic vinegar
5ml/1 tsp lemon juice
chopped fresh mixed herbs
salt and freshly ground black pepper

SERVES 4

1 Cut the peppers in half and remove the seeds and stalks. Cut into quarters and cook, skin side down, over a hot barbecue or grill until the skin chars. Transfer to a bowl and leave to cool. Peel the peppers and cut into strips.

2 Arrange the peppers and fresh tomatoes on a serving dish. Scatter over the anchovies, sun-dried tomatoes, capers, pine nuts and garlic.

3 To make the dressing, mix together the olive oil, vinegar, lemon juice and chopped fresh herbs and season with plenty of salt and pepper. Pour the dressing over the salad before serving.

SWEET AND SOUR ONION SALAD

. . .

This recipe for tangy, glazed onions in the Provençal style makes an unusual and flavourful
accompaniment to barbecued steaks.

INGREDIENTS
450g/1lb baby onions, peeled
50ml/2fl oz/¼ cup wine vinegar
45ml/3 tbsp olive oil
40g/1½ oz/3 tbsp caster sugar
45ml/3 tbsp tomato purée
1 bay leaf
2 parsley sprigs
65g/2½ oz/½ cup raisins
salt and freshly ground black
pepper

SERVES 6

1 Put all the ingredients in a pan with 300ml/½ pint/1¼ cups water. Bring to the boil and simmer gently, uncovered, for 45 minutes, or until the onions are tender and the liquid has evaporated.

2 Remove the bay leaf and parsley, from the pan and check the seasoning. Transfer the contents of the pan to a large serving dish. Serve the salad at room temperature.

SALADS AND ACCOMPANIMENTS

CHORIZO IN OLIVE OIL

· · ·

*Spanish chorizo sausage has a deliciously pungent taste. Frying chorizo with onions and olive oil
is one of the best ways of using it; you can also cook it on the barbecue, brushed with olive oil.*

INGREDIENTS

*75ml/5 tbsp extra virgin olive oil
350g/12oz chorizo sausage, sliced
1 large onion, thinly sliced
flat leaf parsley, roughly chopped,
to garnish*

SERVES 4

1 Heat the olive oil in a frying pan
and fry the chorizo sausage over a high
heat until beginning to colour. Remove
from the pan with a slotted spoon.

2 Add the onion slices to the pan and
fry until golden. Return the sausage
slices to the pan to heat through for
about 1 minute.

3 Tip the mixture into a shallow
serving dish and scatter with the
roughly chopped flat-leaf parsley.
Serve the chorizo on its own or as
a side dish, with warm crusty bread.

Variation

Chorizo is usually available
in large supermarkets and
delicatessens, but any other
similar spicy sausage can be
used as a substitute.

BROAD BEAN, MUSHROOM AND CHORIZO SALAD

· · ·

*This salad can be served as a first course or as part of a buffet menu. Prepare it a day
in advance and store it in the fridge until needed.*

INGREDIENTS

225g/8oz shelled broad beans
175g/6oz chorizo sausage
60ml/4 tbsp extra virgin olive oil
*225g/8oz brown cap mushrooms,
sliced*
handful of fresh chives
*salt and freshly ground black
pepper*

SERVES 4

1 Cook the broad beans in a large
saucepan of boiling, salted water until
just tender. Drain and refresh under
cold running water. If the beans are
large, peel away the tough outer skins.

2 Remove the skin from the chorizo
sausage and cut it into small chunks.
Heat the oil in a frying pan, add the
chorizo and cook for 2 minutes. Empty
into a bowl with the mushrooms, mix
well and leave aside to cool.

3 Chop half the chives and stir the
beans and chopped chives into the
mushroom mixture. Season to taste.
Serve the salad at room temperature,
garnished with the remaining chives.

185

SALSAS, DIPS AND MARINADES

—◆—

The powerful flavours of barbecued meat and fish call for spicy,

lively accompaniments. Chunky salsas are ideal, with their

intriguing combination of cool, crisp ingredients and fiery flavours.

Tangy barbecue sauce is a more traditional alternative that children

adore. For a subtler effect, melt a pat of butter flavoured with herbs,

garlic or anchovies over a plainly grilled steak or fish. This chapter

also includes some appetizing dips to go with crisps, bread sticks

and crudités, and a selection of delicious marinades suitable for

a wide variety of meat and fish.

CHUNKY CHERRY TOMATO SALSA

Succulent cherry tomatoes and refreshing cucumber form the base of this delicious dill-seasoned salsa. Prepare up to 1 day in advance and store in the fridge until needed.

INGREDIENTS

1 ridge cucumber
5ml/1 tsp sea salt
500g/1¼ lb cherry tomatoes
grated rind and juice of 1 lemon
45ml/3 tbsp chilli oil
2.5ml/½ tsp dried chilli flakes
30ml/2 tbsp chopped fresh dill
1 garlic clove, finely chopped
salt and freshly ground black
pepper

SERVES 4

1 Trim the ends off the cucumber and cut it into 2.5cm/1in lengths, then cut each piece lengthways into thin slices. Place in a colander and sprinkle with sea salt. Leave for 5 minutes.

2 Rinse the cucumber slices under cold water and dry with kitchen paper.

3 Quarter the cherry tomatoes and place in a bowl with the cucumber.

4 Whisk together the lemon rind and juice, chilli oil, chilli flakes, dill and garlic. Season, then pour over the tomato and cucumber and toss well. Marinate for 2 hours before serving.

Cook's Tip
Try flavouring the salsa with other herbs: tarragon, coriander or mint.

SALSA VERDE
· · ·

There are many versions of this classic green salsa. Try this one drizzled over char-grilled squid, or with jacket potatoes.

INGREDIENTS

2–4 green chillies, halved
8 spring onions
2 garlic cloves
50g/2oz salted capers
sprig of fresh tarragon
bunch of fresh parsley
grated rind and juice of 1 lime
juice of 1 lemon
90ml/6 tbsp olive oil
about 15ml/1 tbsp green Tabasco
sauce, to taste
freshly ground black pepper

SERVES 4

1 Seed the chillies and trim the spring onions. Halve the garlic cloves. Place in a food processor and pulse briefly.

2 Use your fingers to rub the excess salt off the capers. Add them, with the tarragon and parsley, to the food processor and pulse again until the ingredients are quite finely chopped.

3 Transfer the mixture to a large bowl. Mix in the lime rind and juice, lemon juice and olive oil, stirring lightly so the citrus juice and oil do not emulsify.

4 Add green Tabasco sauce, a little at a time, and black pepper to taste. Chill the salsa in the fridge until ready to serve, but do not prepare it more than 8 hours in advance.

FIERY CITRUS SALSA

This unusual salsa makes a fantastic marinade for shellfish and it is also delicious drizzled over barbecued meat.

INGREDIENTS

1 orange
1 green apple
2 fresh red chillies
1 garlic clove
8 fresh mint leaves
juice of 1 lemon
salt and freshly ground black
pepper

SERVES 4

1 Using a sharp knife, remove the peel and pith from the orange and, working over a bowl to catch the juices, cut out the segments. Squeeze any remaining juice into the bowl.

2 Use a sharp kitchen knife to peel the apple and slice it into wedges. Remove and discard the apple core.

3 Halve the chillies and remove the seeds, then place them in a blender or food processor with the orange segments and juice, apple wedges, garlic and mint.

4 Process until smooth. With the motor running, slowly pour in the lemon juice. Season to taste with salt and freshly ground black pepper and serve immediately.

BARBECUED SWEETCORN SALSA
⋄ ⋄ ⋄

Serve this succulent salsa with grilled gammon or pork, or with smoked meats. The char-grilled corn cob makes the salsa particularly flavoursome.

INGREDIENTS

2 corn cobs
30ml/2 tbsp melted butter
4 tomatoes
6 spring onions, finely chopped
1 garlic clove, finely chopped
30ml/2 tbsp lemon juice
30ml/2 tbsp olive oil
red Tabasco sauce, to taste
salt and freshly ground black pepper

SERVES 4

3 Skewer the tomatoes and hold over the barbecue or grill for about 2 minutes, turning, until the skin splits and wrinkles. Slip off the skins and dice the flesh. Add to the sweetcorn with the spring onions and chopped garlic.

4 Stir the lemon juice and olive oil together, adding Tabasco, salt and black pepper to taste. Pour over the salsa, stir well, cover and leave to marinate at room temperature for 1–2 hours before serving.

1 Remove the husks and silks from the corn cobs. Brush with the melted butter and gently barbecue or grill them for about 20 minutes, turning occasionally, until tender and charred.

2 To remove the kernels, stand each cob upright on a chopping board and use a large, heavy knife to slice down the length of the cob. Put the kernels in a mixing bowl.

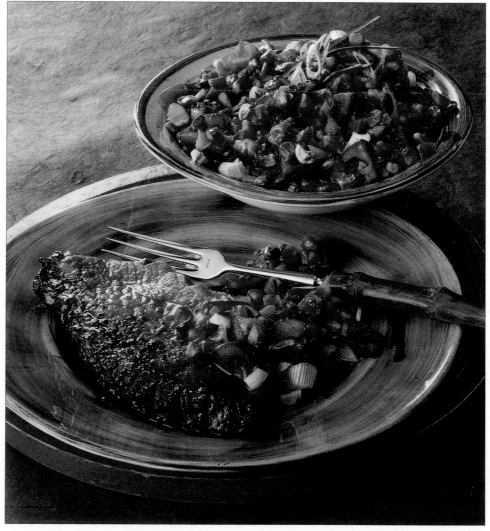

BARBECUE SAUCE

Brush this sauce liberally over chicken drumsticks, chops or kebabs before cooking on the barbecue, or serve as a hot or cold accompaniment to hot dogs and burgers.

INGREDIENTS

30ml/2 tbsp vegetable oil
1 large onion, chopped
2 garlic cloves, crushed
400g/14oz can tomatoes
30ml/2 tbsp Worcestershire sauce
15ml/1 tbsp white wine vinegar
45ml/3 tbsp honey
5ml/1 tsp mustard powder
2.5ml/½ tsp chilli seasoning or mild chilli powder
salt and freshly ground black pepper

SERVES 4

3 Pour into a food processor or blender and process until smooth.

4 Press through a sieve if you prefer. Adjust the seasoning to taste.

1 Heat the vegetable oil in a large saucepan and fry the onions and garlic until soft and golden.

2 Stir in the remaining ingredients and simmer, uncovered, for about 15–20 minutes, stirring occasionally. Remove the saucepan from the heat and allow to cool slightly.

GUACAMOLE

. . .

Nachos or tortilla chips are the classic accompaniments for this classic Mexican dip, but it also tastes great served on the side with burgers or kebabs.

INGREDIENTS

2 ripe avocados
2 red chillies, seeded
1 garlic clove
1 shallot
30ml/2 tbsp olive oil, plus
extra to serve
juice of 1 lemon
salt
fresh flat leaf parsley, to garnish

SERVES 4

1 Halve the avocados, flick out the stones, using the point of a sharp knife, and use a dessert spoon to scoop the flesh into a large bowl.

2 Mash the flesh well, using a potato masher or a large fork, so that the avocado is a fairly smooth consistency.

3 Finely chop the chillies, garlic clove and shallot, then stir into the mashed avocado with the olive oil and lemon juice. Add salt to taste and mix well.

4 Spoon the mixture into a serving bowl. Drizzle over a little more olive oil and scatter with flat leaf parsley leaves. Serve immediately. Guacamole will not keep for very long but can be prepared up to 8 hours in advance and stored in the fridge, sprinkled with lemon juice and covered with clear film.

195

CREAMY AUBERGINE DIP

*Spread this velvet-textured dip thickly on to slices of French bread toasted on the barbecue,
then top with slivers of sun-dried tomato to make wonderful Italian-style crostini.*

INGREDIENTS

1 large aubergine
30ml/2 tbsp olive oil
1 small onion, finely chopped
2 garlic cloves, finely chopped
60ml/4 tbsp chopped fresh parsley
75ml/5 tbsp crème fraîche
red Tabasco sauce, to taste
juice of 1 lemon, to taste
*salt and freshly ground black
pepper*

SERVES 4

3 Peel the aubergine and mash the
flesh with a large fork or potato masher
to make a pulpy purée.

4 Stir in the onion and garlic, parsley
and crème fraîche. Add Tabasco, lemon
juice, and season to taste. Serve warm.

1 Cook the whole aubergine on
a medium barbecue or grill for about
20 minutes, turning occasionally, until
the skin is blackened and the aubergine
soft. Cover the aubergine with a clean
dish towel and set aside to cool for
about 5–6 minutes.

2 Heat the oil in a frying pan and
cook the chopped onion and garlic for
5 minutes, until soft but not browned.

FAT-FREE SAFFRON DIP

Serve this mild dip with fresh vegetable crudités – it is particularly good with florets of cauliflower, asparagus tips and baby carrots and corn.

INGREDIENTS

15ml/1 tbsp boiling water
small pinch saffron strands
200g/7oz/scant 1 cup fat-free fromage frais
10 fresh chives
10 fresh basil leaves
salt and freshly ground black pepper

SERVES 4

1 Pour the boiling water into a bowl and add the saffron strands. Leave to infuse for 3 minutes.

2 Beat the fromage frais in a large bowl until smooth. Stir in the infused saffron liquid with a wooden spoon.

Cook's Tip

If you don't have any saffron, add a squeeze of lemon or lime juice.

3 Snip the chives into the dip. Tear the basil leaves into small pieces and stir them in. Mix thoroughly.

4 Add salt and freshly ground black pepper to taste. Serve the dip with fresh vegetable crudités, if liked.

CHAR-GRILLED APPLES ON CINNAMON TOASTS

· · ·

This simple, scrumptious dessert is best made with an enriched bread such as brioche,
but any light sweet bread will do.

INGREDIENTS

4 sweet, dessert apples
juice of ½ lemon
4 individual brioches or muffins
60ml/4 tbsp melted butter
30ml/2 tbsp golden caster sugar
5ml/1 tsp ground cinnamon
whipped cream or Greek-style
yogurt, to serve

SERVES 4

2 Cut the brioches or muffins into thick slices. Brush the slices with melted butter on both sides.

4 Place the apple and brioche slices on a medium-hot barbecue and cook them for about 3–4 minutes, turning once, until they are beginning to turn golden brown. Do not allow to burn.

1 Core the apples and use a sharp knife to cut them into 3–4 thick slices. Sprinkle the apple slices with lemon juice and set them aside.

3 Mix together the caster sugar and ground cinnamon in a small bowl to make the cinnamon sugar. Set aside.

5 Sprinkle half the cinnamon sugar over the apple slices and brioche toasts and cook for a further minute on the barbecue, until the sugar is sizzling and the toasts are a rich golden brown.

6 To serve, arrange the apple slices over the toasts and sprinkle them with the remaining cinnamon sugar. Serve hot, with whipped cream or Greek-style yogurt, if liked.

PINEAPPLE WEDGES WITH RUM BUTTER GLAZE
· · ·

*Fresh pineapple is even more full of flavour when barbecued, and this spiced rum glaze
makes it into a very special dessert.*

INGREDIENTS

1 medium pineapple
30ml/2 tbsp dark muscovado sugar
5ml/1 tsp ground ginger
60ml/4 tbsp melted butter
30ml/2 tbsp dark rum

SERVES 4

3 Soak 4 bamboo skewers in
water for 15 minutes to prevent them
scorching on the barbecue. Push a
skewer through each wedge, into the
stalk, to hold the chunks in place.

4 Mix together the sugar, ginger,
butter and rum and brush over the
pineapple. Cook the wedges on the
barbecue for 4 minutes; pour the
remaining glaze over the top and serve.

1 With a large, sharp knife, cut the
pineapple lengthways into four wedges.
Cut out and discard the central core.

2 Cut between the flesh and skin,
to release the skin, but leave the flesh
in place. Slice the flesh across and
lengthways to make thick chunks.

Cook's Tip

For an easier version, simply
remove the skin and then cut the
whole pineapple into thick slices
and cook as above.

BAKED BANANAS WITH SPICY VANILLA FILLING
· · ·

Bananas are ideal for barbecue cooking as they bake in their skins and need no preparation at all. This flavoured butter adds richness; children may prefer melted chocolate, jam or honey.

INGREDIENTS

4 bananas
6 green cardamom pods
1 vanilla pod
finely grated rind of 1 small orange
30ml/2 tbsp brandy or orange juice
60ml/4 tbsp light muscovado sugar
45ml/3 tbsp butter
crème fraîche or Greek-style yogurt, to serve

SERVES 4

1 Place the bananas, in their skins, on a hot barbecue and leave for 6–8 minutes, turning occasionally, until they are turning brownish-black.

2 Meanwhile, split the cardamom pods and remove the seeds. Crush lightly in a pestle and mortar.

3 Split the vanilla pod lengthways and scrape out the tiny seeds. Mix with the cardamom seeds, orange rind, brandy or juice, muscovado sugar and butter into a thick paste.

4 Using a sharp knife, slit the skin of each banana, then open out the skin and spoon in a little of the paste. Serve with a spoonful of crème fraîche or Greek-style yogurt, if liked.

ORANGES IN MAPLE AND COINTREAU SYRUP

*This is one of the most delicious ways to eat an orange, and a luxurious way to round off
a barbecued meal. For a children's or alcohol-free version, omit the liqueur.*

INGREDIENTS

*20ml/4 tsp butter, plus extra,
melted, for brushing
4 medium oranges
30 ml/2 tbsp maple syrup
30ml/2 tbsp Cointreau or Grand
Marnier liqueur
crème fraîche or fromage frais,
to serve*

SERVES 4

2 Remove some shreds of orange rind, to decorate. Blanch these, dry them and set them aside. Peel the oranges, removing all the white pith and catching the juice in a bowl.

3 Slice the oranges crossways into thick slices. Reassemble them and place each orange on a square of baking foil.

4 Tuck the baking foil up securely around the oranges to keep them in shape, leaving the foil open at the top.

5 Mix together the reserved orange juice, maple syrup and liqueur and spoon the mixture over the oranges.

1 Cut four double-thickness squares of baking foil, large enough to wrap each of the oranges. Brush the centre of each square of foil with plenty of melted butter.

6 Add a knob of butter to each parcel and close the foil at the top to seal in the juices. Place the parcels on a hot barbecue for 10–12 minutes, until hot. Serve with crème fraîche or fromage frais, topped with the reserved shreds of orange rind.

GRIDDLE CAKES WITH MULLED PLUMS

. . .

*These delectably light little pancakes are fun to make on the barbecue. They are served with
a rich, spicy plum sauce.*

INGREDIENTS

500g/1¼ lb red plums
90ml/6 tbsp light muscovado sugar
1 cinnamon stick
2 whole cloves
1 piece star anise
90ml/6 tbsp apple juice
*cream or Greek-style yogurt,
to serve*

FOR THE GRIDDLE CAKES
50g/2oz/½ cup plain flour
10ml/2 tsp baking powder
pinch of salt
50g/2oz/½ cup fine cornmeal
30ml/2 tbsp light muscovado sugar
1 egg, beaten
300ml/½ pint/1¼ cups milk
30ml/2 tbsp corn oil

SERVES 6

1 Halve, stone and quarter the
plums. Place them in a flameproof pan,
with the sugar, spices and apple juice.

Cook's Tip

If you prefer, make the
griddle cakes in advance, on
the hob, and then simply heat
them for a few seconds on the
barbecue to serve with the plums.

2 Bring to the boil, then reduce the
heat, cover the pan and simmer gently
for 8–10 minutes, stirring occasionally,
until the plums are soft. Remove the
spices and keep the plums warm on
the side of the barbecue.

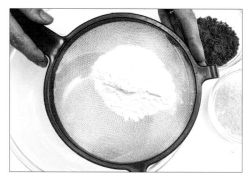

3 For the griddle cakes, sift the
plain flour, baking powder and salt
into a large mixing bowl and stir in
the cornmeal and muscovado sugar.

4 Make a well in the centre of
the ingredients and add the egg, then
beat in the milk. Beat thoroughly with
a whisk or wooden spoon to form a
smooth batter. Beat in half the oil.

5 Heat a griddle or a heavy frying
pan on a hot barbecue. Brush with the
remaining oil, then drop tablespoons
of batter on to it, allowing them to
spread. Cook the griddle cakes for
about a minute, until bubbles start
to appear on the surface and the
underside is golden brown.

6 Turn the cakes over and cook the
other side for a further minute, or until
golden. Serve the cakes hot from the
griddle with a spoonful of mulled
plums and cream or yogurt.

FRESH FIGS WITH VANILLA CREAM

. . .

The ripeness of the figs will determine their cooking time. This is an ideal recipe for a barbecue because it is prepared on the barbecue and left to stand until you are ready to eat.

INGREDIENTS

450ml/³/₄ pint/scant 2 cups dry white wine
75g/3oz/¹/₃ cup clear honey
50g/2oz/¹/₄ cup caster sugar
1 small orange
8 whole cloves
450g/1lb fresh figs
1 cinnamon stick
sprigs of fresh mint, or bay leaves, to decorate

FOR THE VANILLA CREAM
300ml/¹/₂ pint/1¹/₄ cups double cream
1 vanilla pod
5ml/1 tsp caster sugar

SERVES 6

1 Put the wine, honey and caster sugar in a heavy saucepan and heat gently on the barbecue or hob until the sugar dissolves.

2 Stud the orange with the cloves and add to the syrup with the figs and cinnamon. Cover and simmer very gently for 5–10 minutes until the figs are tender. Transfer the contents of the pan to a serving dish and leave to cool.

3 Put 150ml/¹/₄ pint/²/₃ cup of the cream in a small saucepan with the vanilla pod. Bring almost to the boil, then leave to cool and infuse for 30 minutes. Remove the vanilla pod and mix the flavoured cream with the remaining cream and sugar in a bowl. Whip lightly. Transfer to a serving dish.

4 Decorate the figs with mint or bay leaves and serve with the vanilla cream.

Baked Apples in Honey and Lemon

• • •

Tender baked apples with a classic flavouring of lemon and honey make a simple dessert.
Serve with custard or a spoonful of whipped cream, if you wish.

INGREDIENTS
4 medium cooking apples
15ml/1 tbsp honey
grated rind and juice of 1 lemon
15ml/1 tbsp butter, melted

SERVES 4

1 Remove the cores from the apples, leaving them whole. Cut four squares of double-thickness baking foil, to wrap the apples, and brush with butter.

2 With a cannelle or sharp knife, cut lines through the apple skin at regular intervals.

3 Mix together the honey, lemon rind, juice and butter in a small bowl.

4 Spoon the mixture into the apples and wrap in foil, sealing the edges securely. Cook on a hot barbecue for 20 minutes, until the apples are tender

221

OUTDOOR ENTERTAINING

Everything tastes better out of doors, and picnics – whether in the garden, at the seaside or in a grassy meadow – are a great pleasure both to organize and to take part in, as long as the weather is kind. If you have a portable barbecue you can take it along with you and make the food twice as exciting, but take care that you light it in a safe place and clear up carefully afterwards. Food for barbecuing can be transported in its marinade, all ready to be popped on to the grill. Pack interesting dips into plastic boxes, and take pittas or prepared vegetables to go with them. Homemade quiches and pies will also help to satisfy healthy outdoor appetites. This section also offers inspirations for special summer meals and garden parties at home, including some original and delicious ideas for party drinks.

VEGETABLES WITH TAPENADE AND HERB AIOLI

∘ ∘ ∘

A beautiful platter of summer vegetables served with one or two interesting sauces makes a really appetizing and informal starter, which is perfect for picnics as it can all be prepared in advance.

INGREDIENTS

2 red peppers, cut into wide strips
30ml/2 tbsp olive oil
225g/8oz new potatoes
115g/4oz green beans
225g/8oz baby carrots
225g/8oz young asparagus
12 quails' eggs
fresh herbs, to garnish
coarse salt, for sprinkling

FOR THE TAPENADE
175g/6oz/1½ cups stoned black olives
50g/2oz can anchovy fillets, drained
30ml/2 tbsp capers
120ml/4fl oz/½ cup olive oil
finely grated rind of 1 lemon
15ml/1 tbsp brandy (optional)
freshly ground black pepper

FOR THE HERB AIOLI
5 garlic cloves, crushed
2 egg yolks
5ml/1 tsp Dijon mustard
10ml/2 tsp white wine vinegar
250ml/8fl oz/1 cup light olive oil
45ml/3 tbsp chopped mixed fresh herbs, such as chervil, parsley and tarragon
30ml/2 tbsp chopped watercress
salt and freshly ground black pepper

SERVES 6

1 To make the tapenade, finely chop the olives, anchovies and capers and beat together with the oil, lemon rind and brandy, if using. (Alternatively, lightly process the ingredients in a blender or food processor.)

2 Season with pepper and blend in a little more oil if the mixture seems very dry. Transfer to a serving dish.

3 To make the aïoli, beat together the garlic, egg yolks, mustard and vinegar. Gradually blend in the olive oil, a drop at a time, whisking well until thick and smooth.

4 Stir in the mixed herbs and watercress. Season with salt and pepper to taste, adding a little more vinegar if necessary. Cover with clear film and chill until ready to serve.

Cook's Tip

Any leftover tapenade is delicious tossed with pasta or spread on to warm toast. If you are making this dish as part of a picnic, allow the vegetables to cool before packing in an airtight container. Pack the quails' eggs in their original box.

5 Brush the peppers with oil and grill on a hot barbecue or under a hot grill until just beginning to char.

6 Cook the potatoes in a large pan of boiling, salted water until tender. Add the beans and carrots and blanch for 1 minute. Add the asparagus and cook for a further 30 seconds. Drain the vegetables. Cook the quails' eggs in boiling water for 2 minutes.

7 Arrange all the vegetables, eggs and sauces on a serving platter. Garnish with fresh herbs and serve with coarse salt, for sprinkling.

CRUDITES

. . .

*Serve a colourful selection of raw vegetables as a quick and easy accompaniment
to apéritif drinks or as a refreshing starter for summer meals.*

RAW VEGETABLE PLATTER

INGREDIENTS

2 red or yellow peppers, sliced
lengthways
225g/8oz fresh baby corn,
blanched
1 chicory head (red or white),
trimmed and leaves separated
175–225g/6–8oz thin asparagus,
trimmed and blanched
small bunch radishes, trimmed
175g/6oz cherry tomatoes
12 quail's eggs, boiled for
3 minutes, drained, refreshed and
peeled
aioli or tapenade,
for dipping

SERVES 6–8

Arrange a selection of prepared
vegetables, chosen from the list above,
on a serving plate with your chosen
dip. Keep covered until ready to serve.

TOMATO AND CUCUMBER SALAD

INGREDIENTS

1 medium cucumber, peeled and
thinly sliced
30ml/2 tbsp white wine vinegar
90ml/3fl oz/⅓ cup crème fraîche or
soured cream
30ml/2 tbsp chopped fresh mint
4 or 5 ripe tomatoes, sliced
salt and freshly ground black
pepper

SERVES 4–6

Place the cucumber in a bowl, sprinkle
with a little salt and 15ml/1 tbsp of the
vinegar and toss with 5 or 6 ice cubes.
Chill for 1 hour to crisp, then rinse,
drain and pat dry. Return to the bowl,
add the cream, pepper and mint and
stir to mix well. Arrange the tomato
slices on a serving plate, sprinkle with
the remaining vinegar, and spoon the
cucumber slices into the centre.

Cook's Tip

Any leftover vegetables can
be used in soups or stir-fries,
even if they have already
been dressed.

CARROT AND ORANGE SALAD

INGREDIENTS

1 garlic clove, crushed
grated rind and juice of 1 unwaxed
orange
30–45ml/2–3 tbsp groundnut oil
450g/1lb carrots, cut into very fine
julienne strips
30–45ml/2–3 tbsp chopped fresh
parsley
salt and freshly ground black
pepper

SERVES 4–6

Rub around a bowl with the garlic
clove, leaving the clove in the bowl.
Add the orange rind and juice, and
season with salt and freshly ground
pepper. Whisk in the groundnut oil
until blended, then remove the garlic
clove. Add the carrots and half of the
fresh parsley and toss well to mix.
Garnish with the remaining parsley.

AIOLI
Put 4 peeled garlic cloves (more or less can be added, to taste) in a bowl with a pinch of salt, and crush with the back of a spoon. Add 2 egg yolks and beat for 30 seconds with an electric mixer until creamy. Beat in 250ml/8fl oz/ 1 cup extra virgin olive oil, drop by drop. As the mixture thickens, the oil can be added in a thin stream. Thin the sauce with lemon juice, if necessary,

and season to taste. Chill for up to 2 days; bring to room temperature and stir before serving.

TAPENADE
Put 200g/7oz stoned black olives, 6 anchovy fillets, 30ml/2 tbsp capers, rinsed, 1 or 2 garlic cloves, 5ml/1 tsp fresh thyme, 15ml/1 tbsp Dijon mustard, the juice of half a lemon, freshly ground black pepper and, if

FROM TOP LEFT: *raw vegetable platter with aïoli, carrot and orange salad, tomato and cucumber salad.*

you like, 15ml/1 tbsp brandy in a food processor and process for about 15–30 seconds until smooth, scraping down the sides of the bowl. With the machine running, pour in 60–90ml/4–6 tbsp extra virgin olive oil to make a smooth paste. Store in an airtight container.

229

FALAFEL

· · ·

These North African fritters are traditionally made using dried broad beans, but chick-peas are more easily available. Serve in warmed pitta bread, with salad and garlicky yogurt.

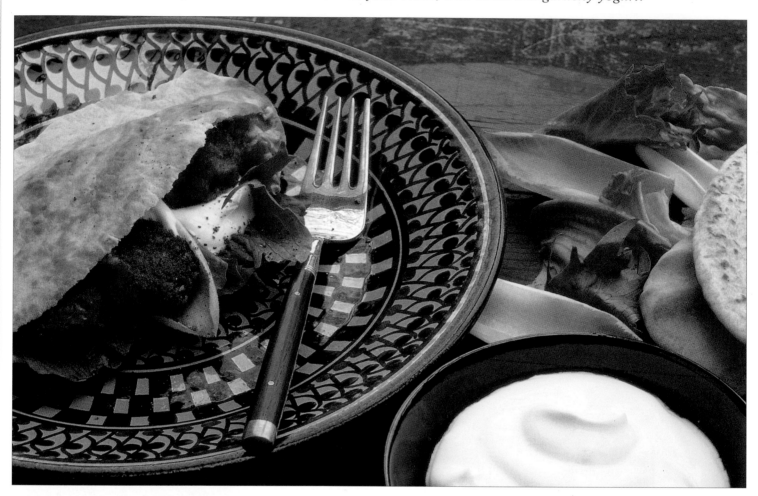

INGREDIENTS

150g/5oz/³⁄4 cup dried chick-peas
1 large onion, roughly chopped
2 garlic cloves, roughly chopped
60ml/4 tbsp roughly chopped fresh parsley
5ml/1 tsp cumin seeds, crushed
5ml/1 tsp coriander seeds, crushed
2.5ml/¹⁄2 tsp baking powder
salt and freshly ground black pepper
oil for deep frying

SERVES 4

1 Put the chick-peas in a large bowl and cover with plenty of cold water. Leave to soak overnight.

2 Drain the chick-peas and cover with fresh water in a saucepan. Bring to the boil and boil rapidly for 10 minutes. Reduce the heat and simmer for about 1 hour, or until soft. Drain.

3 Place in a food processor with the onion, garlic, parsley, cumin, coriander and baking powder. Season to taste. Process to form a firm paste.

4 Shape the mixture into walnut-size balls, using your hands, and flatten them slightly. In a deep pan, heat 5cm/2in oil until a little of the mixture sizzles on the surface. Fry the falafel in batches until golden. Drain on kitchen paper and serve.

Cook's Tip
Although they can be fried in advance, falafel are at their best served warm. Wrap them in foil or pack them in an insulated container to take them on picnics, or keep them warm on the edge of the barbecue until needed.

HUMMUS BI TAHINA

Blending chick-peas with garlic, lemon and oil makes a deliciously creamy purée to serve as a dip with crudités or warmed pitta bread.

INGREDIENTS

150g/5oz/¾ cup dried chick-peas
juice of 2 lemons
2 garlic cloves, sliced
30ml/2 tbsp olive oil, plus extra to serve
150ml/¼ pint/⅔ cup tahini paste
salt and freshly ground black pepper
cayenne pepper, to serve
flat leaf parsley, to garnish

SERVES 4–6

1 Put the chick-peas in a large bowl and cover with plenty of cold water. Leave to soak overnight.

2 Drain the chick-peas and cover with fresh water in a pan. Bring to the boil and boil rapidly for 10 minutes. Reduce the heat and simmer for about 1 hour, or until soft. Drain.

3 Process the chick-peas to a purée in a food processor. Add lemon juice, garlic, oil, cayenne pepper and tahini and blend until creamy.

4 Season the chick-pea purée with plenty of salt and freshly ground black pepper and transfer to a serving dish. Drizzle the purée with olive oil and sprinkle lightly with cayenne pepper. Serve the dip garnished with a few flat leaf parsley sprigs.

Cook's Tip

If you do not have time to soak dried chick-peas, canned chick-peas can be used instead. Allow two 400g/14oz cans and drain them thoroughly.

TOMATO AND CHEESE TARTS

These crisp little tartlets look impressive but are actually very easy to make.
They are best eaten fresh from the oven.

INGREDIENTS
3 sheets filo pastry
1 egg white
175g/6oz cream cheese
handful fresh basil leaves
4 small tomatoes, sliced
salt and freshly ground black
pepper

MAKES 12

1 Preheat the oven to 200°C/400°F/
Gas 6. Brush the sheets of filo pastry
lightly with egg white and cut into
24 × 10cm/4in squares.

2 Layer the squares in twos, in
12 bun tins. Spoon the cream cheese
into the pastry cases. Season with
ground black pepper and top with
fresh basil leaves.

3 Arrange the tomatoes on the tarts,
season and bake for 10–12 minutes,
until the pastry is golden. Serve warm.

Cook's Tip
Use halved cherry tomatoes
for the tarts, if you prefer.

TANDOORI CHICKEN STICKS

These aromatic chicken pieces are traditionally baked in the special clay oven known as a tandoor. They are equally delicious served hot or cold, and make irresistible barbecue food.

INGREDIENTS

450g/1lb boneless, skinless chicken breasts

FOR THE CORIANDER YOGURT
250ml/8fl oz/1 cup natural yogurt
30ml/2 tbsp whipping cream
½ cucumber, peeled, seeded and finely chopped
15–30ml/1–2 tbsp fresh chopped coriander or mint
salt and freshly ground black pepper

FOR THE MARINADE
175ml/6fl oz/¾ cup natural yogurt
5ml/1 tsp garam masala or curry powder
1.5ml/¼ tsp ground cumin
1.5ml/¼ tsp ground coriander
1.5ml/¼ tsp cayenne pepper (or to taste)
5ml/1 tsp tomato purée
1–2 garlic cloves, finely chopped
2.5cm/1in piece fresh root ginger, finely chopped
grated zest and juice of ½ lemon
15–30ml/1–2 tbsp fresh chopped coriander or mint

MAKES ABOUT 25

2 To prepare the marinade, place all the ingredients in a food processor and process until smooth. Pour into a shallow dish.

3 Freeze the chicken breasts for 5 minutes to firm them, then slice in half horizontally. Cut the slices into 2cm/¾ in strips and add to the marinade. Toss to coat well. Cover with clear film and chill for 6–8 hours or overnight.

4 Drain the chicken pieces and arrange on a rack, scrunching up the chicken slightly to make wavy shapes. Cook on a hot barbecue for 4–5 minutes until brown and cooked through, turning once. Alternatively, arrange on a foil-lined baking sheet and cook under a hot grill. Serve hot, threaded on cocktail sticks or short skewers, with the yogurt dip. For a picnic, cool and pack into a box.

1 For the coriander yogurt, combine all the ingredients in a bowl. Season, cover and chill until ready to serve.

HAM PIZZETTAS WITH MELTED BRIE AND MANGO

These individual little pizzas are topped with an unusual but very successful combination of smoked ham, Brie and juicy chunks of fresh mango.

INGREDIENTS

225g/8oz/2 cups strong white flour
10g/¼ oz sachet easy-blend dried yeast
150ml/¼ pint/⅔ cup warm water
60ml/4 tbsp olive oil

FOR THE TOPPING
1 ripe mango
150g/5oz smoked ham, sliced wafer-thin
150g/5oz Brie cheese, diced
12 yellow cherry tomatoes, halved
salt and freshly ground black pepper

SERVES 6

2 Turn the dough out on to a floured surface and knead it for about 5 minutes, or until smooth.

3 Return the dough to the bowl and cover it with a damp cloth or oiled clear film. Leave the dough to prove in a warm place for about 30 minutes or until the dough is doubled in size and springy to the touch.

4 Divide the dough into six and roll each piece into a ball. Flatten out with your hand and use your knuckles to press each piece of dough to a round of about 15cm/6in diameter, with a raised lip around the edge.

5 Halve, stone and peel the mango and cut it into small dice. Arrange with the ham on top of the pizzettas. Top with cheese and tomatoes and sprinkle with salt and ground black pepper.

1 In a large bowl, stir together the flour and yeast, with a pinch of salt. Make a well in the centre and stir in the water and 45ml/3 tbsp of the olive oil. Stir until thoroughly mixed.

Cook's Tip

It's important to flatten out the dough rounds quite thinly and to cook them fairly slowly, or they will not cook evenly. To save time, you could use a 300g/11oz packet of pizza dough mix.

6 Drizzle the remaining oil over the pizzettas. Place them on a medium-hot barbecue and cook for 8 minutes, until golden brown and crisp underneath.

MEDITERRANEAN QUICHE

. . .

This quiche forms the ideal base for a hearty picnic feast. The strong Mediterranean flavours of tomatoes, peppers and anchovies complement the cheese pastry beautifully.

INGREDIENTS

FOR THE PASTRY
225g/8oz/2 cups plain flour
pinch of salt
pinch of dry mustard
115g/4oz/½ cup butter, chilled and
diced
50g/2oz Gruyère cheese, grated
salt and freshly ground black
pepper

FOR THE FILLING
50g/2oz can anchovy fillets, drained
50ml/2fl oz/¼ cup milk
30ml/2 tbsp French mustard
45ml/3 tbsp olive oil
2 large Spanish onions, peeled and
sliced
1 red pepper, very finely sliced
3 egg yolks
350ml/12fl oz/1½ cups double
cream
1 garlic clove, crushed
175g/6oz sharp Cheddar cheese,
grated
2 large tomatoes, thickly sliced
30ml/2 tbsp chopped fresh basil, to
garnish

SERVES 6–8

2 Add the Gruyère cheese and process again briefly. Add enough iced water to make a stiff dough: the dough will be ready when it forms a ball. Wrap the dough in clear film and chill in the fridge for at least 30 minutes.

3 Meanwhile, make the filling. Soak the anchovies in the milk for about 20 minutes to make them less salty. Pour off the milk. Heat the olive oil in a frying pan and cook the onions and red pepper until they soften.

4 In a bowl, beat the egg yolks, cream, garlic and Cheddar cheese together; season with salt and pepper.

5 Preheat the oven to 200°C/400°F/ Gas 6. Roll out the chilled pastry and line a 23cm/9in loose-based quiche tin. Spread the mustard over and chill in the fridge for a further 15 minutes.

6 Arrange the tomatoes in a layer in the pastry crust. Top with the onion and pepper mixture and the anchovy fillets. Pour over the egg mixture. Bake for 30 minutes. Serve warm or at room temperature, sprinkled with fresh basil.

Cook's Tip
Leave the quiche in its tin if you are packing it for a picnic.

1 To make the pastry, place the flour, salt and mustard in a food processor, add the butter and process the mixture until it resembles fine breadcrumbs.

CHICKEN AND APRICOT FILO PIE

The filling for this pie has a Middle Eastern flavour – minced chicken combined with apricots, bulgur wheat, nuts and spices. It both looks and tastes spectacular.

INGREDIENTS

75g/3oz/½ cup bulgur wheat
75g/3oz/6 tbsp butter
1 onion, chopped
450g/1lb minced chicken
50g/2oz/¼ cup ready-to-eat dried apricots, finely chopped
25g/1oz/¼ cup blanched almonds, chopped
5ml/1 tsp ground cinnamon
2.5ml/½ tsp ground allspice
50ml/2fl oz/¼ cup Greek yogurt
15ml/1 tbsp snipped fresh chives, plus extra to garnish
30ml/2 tbsp chopped fresh parsley
6 large sheets filo pastry
salt and freshly ground black pepper

SERVES 6

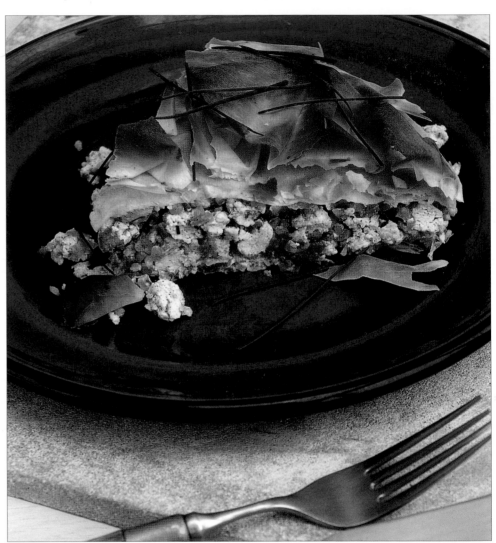

1 Preheat the oven to 200°C/400°F/ Gas 6. Put the bulgur wheat in a large bowl with 120ml/4fl oz/½ cup boiling water. Allow the wheat to soak for 5 minutes, until the water is absorbed.

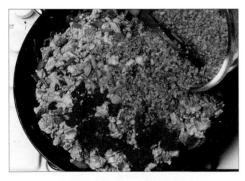

2 Heat 25g/1oz/2 tbsp of the butter in a pan and fry the onion and chicken until pale golden. Stir in the apricots, almonds and bulgur wheat and cook for a further 2 minutes. Remove from the heat and stir in the cinnamon, allspice, yogurt, chives and parsley. Season to taste with salt and pepper.

3 Melt the remaining butter. Unroll the filo pastry and cut into 25cm/10in rounds. Keep the pastry rounds covered with a clean, damp dish towel to prevent them from drying out.

4 Line a 23cm/9in loose-based flan tin with three pastry rounds, brushing each with butter as you layer them. Spoon in the chicken mixture and cover with three more pastry rounds, brushed with melted butter as before.

5 Crumple the remaining rounds and place on top of the pie. Brush with any remaining butter. Bake the pie for about 30 minutes, until the pastry is golden brown and crisp. Serve the pie hot or cold, garnished with fresh chives.

CHICKEN WITH FRESH HERBS AND GARLIC

A whole chicken can be roasted on a spit on the barbecue. This marinade keeps the flesh moist and delicious and the fresh herbs add summery flavours.

INGREDIENTS

1.75kg/4½ lb free-range chicken
finely grated rind and juice of 1
lemon
1 garlic clove, crushed
30ml/2 tbsp olive oil
2 fresh thyme sprigs
2 fresh sage sprigs
90ml/6 tbsp unsalted butter,
softened
salt and freshly ground black
pepper

SERVES 4

1 Season the chicken well. Mix the lemon rind and juice, crushed garlic and olive oil together and pour them over the chicken. Leave to marinate in the fridge for at least 2 hours.

Cook's Tip

If roasting the chicken in the oven, preheat the oven to 230°C/450°F/ Gas 8 and reduce the heat to 190°C/375°F/Gas 5 after 10 minutes. If you are roasting a chicken to serve cold, cooking it in foil helps to keep it succulent – open the foil for the last 20 minutes to brown the skin, then close it as the chicken cools.

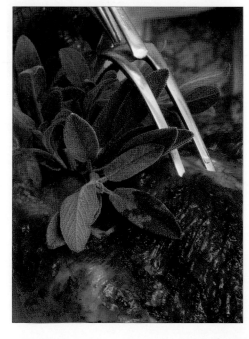

2 Place the herbs in the cavity of the bird and smear the butter over the skin. Season well. Cook the chicken on a spit on the barbecue for 1½–1¾ hours, basting with the marinade, until the juices run clear when the thigh is pierced with a skewer. Leave the bird to rest for 15 minutes before carving.

PEPPER STEAK

. . .

This easy, rather indulgent, bistro classic can be put together in a matter of minutes for an intimate summer supper in the garden. The creamy sauce helps to balance the heat of the pepper.

INGREDIENTS

30ml/2 tbsp black peppercorns
2 fillet or sirloin steaks, about
225g/8oz each
15g/¹/₂ oz/1 tbsp butter
10ml/2 tsp olive oil
45ml/3 tbsp brandy
150ml/1/4 pint/²/₃ cup whipping
cream
1 garlic clove, finely chopped
salt, if necessary

SERVES 2

1 Place the black peppercorns in a sturdy polythene bag. Crush the peppercorns with a rolling pin or steak hammer until they are crushed to medium-coarse pepper.

2 Put the steaks on a chopping board and trim away any excess fat, using a sharp kitchen knife. Press the pepper firmly on to both sides of the meat, to coat it completely.

3 Melt the butter with the olive oil in a heavy frying pan over a medium-high heat. Add the meat and cook for 6–7 minutes, turning once, until cooked to your liking. Transfer the steaks to a warmed platter or plates and cover to keep warm.

4 Pour in the brandy to de-glaze the frying pan. Allow the brandy to boil until it has reduced by half, scraping the base of the frying pan, then add the whipping cream and garlic. Bubble gently over a low-medium heat for about 4 minutes or until the cream has reduced by about one-third. Stir any accumulated juices from the meat into the sauce, taste and add salt as necessary. Serve the steaks hot, with the sauce.

LAMB CASS

This recipe has a S

INGREDIENTS
45ml/3 tbsp olive oil
1.5kg/3–3½ lb lamb fillet, cut
into 5cm/2in cubes
1 large onion, chopped
6 large garlic cloves, unpeeled
1 bay leaf
5ml/1 tsp paprika
120ml/4fl oz/½ cup dry sherry
115g/4oz shelled fresh or froze
broad beans
30ml/2 tbsp chopped fresh parsl
salt and freshly ground black
pepper

SERVES 6

1 Heat 30ml/2 tbsp olive oil in
large flameproof casserole. Add h
the meat and brown well on all si
Transfer to a plate. Brown the res
of the meat in the same way and
remove from the casserole.

2 Heat the remaining oil in the
add the onion and cook for abou
5 minutes until soft. Return the n
to the casserole.

PORK WITH MARSALA AND JUNIPER

. . .

*Sicilian marsala wine gives savoury dishes a rich, fruity and alcoholic tang. The pork is fully
complemented by the flavour of the sauce in this quick and luxurious dish.*

INGREDIENTS
25g/1oz dried cep or porcini
mushrooms
4 pork escalopes
10ml/2 tsp balsamic vinegar
8 garlic cloves
15g/½ oz/1 tbsp butter
45ml/3 tbsp marsala
several rosemary sprigs
10 juniper berries, crushed
salt and freshly ground black
pepper

SERVES 4

1 Put the dried mushrooms in a
large bowl and just cover with hot
water. Leave to stand for 20 minutes
to allow the mushrooms to soak.

2 Brush the pork with 5ml/1 tsp of
the vinegar and season with salt and
pepper. Put the garlic cloves in a small
pan of boiling water and cook for 10
minutes until soft. Drain and set aside.

3 Melt the butter in a large frying
pan. Add the pork and fry quickly until
browned on the underside. Turn the
meat over and cook for 1 minute more.

4 Add the marsala, rosemary sprigs,
drained mushrooms, 60ml/4 tbsp of
the mushroom water, the garlic cloves,
juniper berries and the remaining
balsamic vinegar.

5 Simmer gently for 3–5 minutes
until the pork is cooked through.
Season lightly and serve hot.

*This recipe uses frui...
and is very good s...*

INGREDIENTS

*60ml/4 tbsp olive oil
1 onion, finely chopped
2 garlic cloves, chopped
50g/2oz/1 cup fresh breadcru...
4 ready-to-eat dried figs, cho...
8 stoned green olives, chopp...
25g/1oz/¼ cup flaked almo...
15ml/1 tbsp lemon juice
15ml/1 tbsp chopped fresh pa...
1 egg yolk
900g/2lb boned loin of po...
salt and freshly ground bla...
pepper*

SERVES 4

1 Preheat the oven to 200°C/4...
Gas 6, or prepare the barbecue. ...
45ml/3 tbsp of the oil in a pan, ...
onion and garlic, and cook gent...
softened. Remove the pan from ...
heat and stir in the breadcrumb...
olives, almonds, lemon juice, ch...
fresh parsley and egg yolk. Seas...
taste with salt and ground black...

2 Remove any string from the ...
and unroll the belly flap, cuttin...
any excess fat or meat to enable...
do so. Spread the stuffing over ...
piece and roll it up, starting fro...
thick side. Tie at intervals with ...